# THE SCOUT'S
## CAMPFIRE COOKBOOK
## FOR KIDS

### TIM AND CHRISTINE CONNERS

**FALCON**GUIDES

GUILFORD, CONNECTICUT
HELENA, MONTANA
AN IMPRINT OF GLOBE PEQUOT PRESS

MIX
Paper from
responsible sources
FSC® C005010

**FALCONGUIDES®**

Text design and layout: Maggie Peterson
Acquisitions editor: David Legere
Project editor: Lauren Szalkiewicz

Library of Congress Cataloging-in-Publication Data is available on file.

ISBN 978-0-7627-9721-9

Printed in the United States of America

10 9 8 7 6 5 4 3 2 1

# BENEDICTION

Lifting up his eyes, then, and seeing that a large crowd was coming toward him, Jesus said to Philip, "Where are we to buy bread, so that these people may eat?" One of his disciples said to him, "There is a boy here who has five barley loaves and two fish, but what are they for so many?" Jesus said, "Have the people sit down."

—John 6:5, 8–10 (ESV)

# CONTENTS

# THE THIRTEEN STEPS TO BUILDING A CAMPFIRE

1. Split dead tree limb into fragments and shave one fragment into slivers.

2. Bandage left thumb.

3. Chop other fragments into smaller fragments.

4. Bandage left foot.

5. Make a structure from the slivers (including those embedded in the hand).

6. Light match.

7. Light match.

8. Repeat "A Scout is cheerful" several times, then light match.

A Cub contemplates Step One of the Thirteen Steps. Scott Simerly

9. Apply match to slivers, add wood fragments, and blow gently into base of flames.

10. Apply burn ointment to nose.

11. Once fire is burning, collect more wood.

12. Once fire is burning well, add all remaining firewood.

13. After thunderstorm has passed, repeat the above steps.

—Paul "Torchy" Dunn
Former director of Scout Division, Boy Scouts of America
Courtesy of *Scouting* magazine, March–April 1978

# ACKNOWLEDGMENTS

Many thanks go to Beth Ramsey, of Boy Scouts of America's Supply Group, who inspired this title. John Clark, former managing editor of *Scouting* magazine, and Michael Goldman, now editor of *Scouting, Boy's Life,* and *Eagle's Call* magazines, have helped us stay connected to the master chefs in the Scouting world. John and Michael, you have our gratitude.

The recipes in this book were provided by many talented outdoor Scout chefs, who are well acquainted with the challenges presented by a camp kitchen staffed with younger kids. This book would not have been possible without their ideas and input, and our deep appreciation goes to all of these fine folks. To our top contributors, Donna Pettigrew, Master Trainer with Girl Scouts of Central Indiana, and Kathleen Kirby, Merit Badge Counselor with Boy Scout Troop 33, Central New Jersey Council, we are particularly grateful for the substantial time and energy you've put into freely sharing so many culinary masterpieces.

What acknowledgement would be complete without a tip of the hat to our longtime acquaintance and master recipe tester, Ken Harbison? Nearly every cookbook title of ours to date has benefited in some way from Ken's attention to detail. He is a consummate professional, and, once again, our book is better for it. As always, many thanks, Ken.

Our gratitude goes to Scout leaders Scott Simerly, Allison Rudick, and Beverly Jo Antonini, not only for their excellent recipes, but also for sharing their interesting photography for this book. Special thanks to Allison for providing the information used in appendix C for building a box oven.

Finally, we recognize the very talented crew at FalconGuides/Globe Pequot Press. In particular, warm appreciation goes to our acquisitions editor, David Legere; to the executive editorial director, Steve Culpepper; and to our longtime crony, colleague, and dear friend, Max Phelps, director of outdoor sales. Thanks to you all for these many years of adventure.

# INTRODUCTION

Young Scouts love to cook! To be blunt, this probably has more to do with their infamous fascination with fire and sharp objects than a true desire to create the perfect pancake. But whatever the reason, the ingredients are there for a captive audience, one ready to attempt something that, for many of them, is an entirely new experience in their budding lives.

Scout leaders rarely have a problem in asking the youngsters to lend a hand when it comes time to cook. Now move the kitchen to an outdoor setting, and the magic really begins. Perhaps it's the fresh air, but young Scouts are often ready to bust a gut in their desire to do something, anything, to help. Camping is energizing like that. Add a campfire, along with a healthy dose of hunger-inducing activities, and Scouts of any age inherently know that cooking is a particularly special aspect of camping.

But as eager as the youngsters are to help, they are the ones who naturally tend to have the least experience and who need the most instruction and oversight in the hazardous environment found in any kitchen. And recalling their fascination with fire and sharp objects, therein lies an even greater challenge.

This book is specifically designed to address this problem. However, let it be clear that it wasn't written with the intention that it be handed to a young Scout along with the instruction to "cook something." No cookbook for kids can eliminate the need for proper supervision. So the intent is not to replace the adult's role in the camp kitchen. Indeed, this book won't even necessarily make the end-to-end cooking job easier, given the simple truth that any attempt to engage and teach those with less skill takes more effort than it would to not engage them at all.

Instead, this book's purpose is to nuture in young Scouts a fascination with and respect for the culinary world by emphasizing key techniques, fundamental kitchen science, and the caution required for successful outdoor cooking. For adult leaders willing to make the effort, this book will help to make the process of cooking with young Scouts easier.

To that end, the book puts less emphasis on the more mundane aspects of meal preparation: grocery shopping, the gathering of ingredients and gear, and the post-meal cleanup. These other steps are important for any chef to learn and master. But the teaching of these skills is assumed to be relegated to a later stage of the Scout's maturation and growth, especially through the merit badge advancement process.

As the title suggests, this book is written primarily with kids in mind. "Kid" is an admittedly loose term. But in this book it refers to young chefs, reasonably proficient at reading, but lacking most, if not all, of the skills necessary to function effectively in the outdoor kitchen. Depending on the maturity and scholastic ability of the Scout, this could cover an age range from first grade to high school, keeping in mind that many are the teenagers who would have no clue how to survive lacking a microwave oven.

In the Scouting world, the advancement process helps ensure that Scouts of higher rank are reasonably adept at cooking. So this book can be very valuable in helping Scouts achieve the requirements of their early ranks related to cooking.

What about adult leaders? Reflecting society's growing reliance on prepackaged foods, many adults can be easily outgunned in the kitchen by Scouts who've earned their cooking merit badge. When those same adults find themselves outdoors as Scout leaders, they may need almost as much assistance as the youngsters! So with a nod toward the parents and leaders tasked with cooking in camp, but otherwise befuddled as to how to safely and effectively engage their young charges in the process, the recipes are

Young Scouts love to cook! *Scott Simerly*

written so that adults, regardless of skill level, can tee the recipes up so that the kids can drive them home.

To avoid overwhelming kids in the camp kitchen, the number of ingredients for each recipe is limited to no more than eight. While total cooking time varies by recipe, the actual time required of the kids is never more than one hour. Recipes are arranged in sequential steps, and multi-pot meals are avoided to prevent complicated parallel cooking processes.

A unique feature of this book is the manner in which the recipes are organized, with preparation steps appropriate for young Scouts clearly separated from those that are not. Hazards unique to each recipe are also plainly listed for quick discussion and review before cooking commences.

The manner in which the preparation steps are written is considered appropriate for the majority of the Scouting population. However, the instructions should never be followed blindly without regard to the uniqueness of your situation! Common sense must always be exercised. And supervision must always be present for the duration of the cooking process.

With an eye especially turned toward caution, don't hesitate to forge ahead with your fledgling Scout chefs. Introduce them to the wonderful sense of satisfaction and accomplishment that comes from cooking in the outdoors. And may this book be of assistance as you step up to the challenge.

This Tiger Cub is seriously enjoying the payoff from his hard work. *Scott Simerly*

# USING THIS BOOK

*The Scout's Campfire Cookbook for Kids* is designed as a teaching aid to help adult Scout leaders instruct their young chefs. The focus is on basic techniques and equipment that chefs can expect to use for the recipes in this book. Also emphasized are safety topics that are fundamental to the camp kitchen environment and that all chefs, no matter their age, should understand and respect.

In the heart of the book are found the recipes, with dozens of options spanning all meal categories. The recipes have been selected with both variety and ease of preparation in mind, but the latter requires a bit more explanation. While all the recipes are likely to be considered "easy" from the perspective of an adult accustomed to cooking in camp, not all will be at the same level of simplicity from the vantage of the young chef. This range in challenge is intentional and designed to expose young Scouts to a wide variety of fundamental cooking methods. A cookbook filled exclusively with no-cook recipes would present perhaps the easiest challenge of all, but where would be the fun and fulfillment in that?

Those familiar with the layout of recipes in other titles in the Scout's Cookbook series will note the similarities in style and format. However, there are several new design features to put emphasis on preparation information and notes of caution of particular importance for adults overseeing young chefs in the camp kitchen.

## Reading a Recipe

Not all portions of these recipes will be of interest to young camp chefs. That's because some of the information will be used primary by the adults in planning and preparing for the camping trip or once they arrive at camp.

The focal point in each recipe for young Scouts is those preparation steps that have been clearly marked for them to perform. Once at camp and time to cook, it's assumed that all ingredients will have been gathered in advance by the adults in charge. Each recipe also provides information for the adults regarding any cooking equipment required for use by the Scouts. This allows the young chefs to stay focused on their specific preparation steps.

Recipes are written as succinctly as possible, to provide enough information for the cooking task to be completed without confusion but without getting overly wordy. This "recipe language" takes a little practice to master, and it's helpful to tell Scouts this in advance. It's also important that the Scouts understand that preparation steps should be followed *in order*. They can not skip around! They should also be taught to ask an adult for help with *any* questions they may have.

Because the Scouts will repeatedly refer to the ingredients lists as they work through each recipe, they must learn to interpret a list. Recipe lists are also written for brevity, and the information can be confusing for first time chefs. For instance, a list might call for "2 (6-ounce) cans tomato sauce." To an eight year old, that probably looks like algebra! There are many such nuances in recipe writing that will be clear to some but not to others, and so Scouts should be encouraged to ask whenever they're unsure.

A description of the design principles and main components used in the recipes is presented in the sections that immediately follow. So the Scouts better understand how and why recipes work, it's recommended that leaders review this material with their young chefs prior to cooking in the field.

## Required Ingredients and Equipment

Each recipe includes a list of required ingredients, selected to minimize waste and leftovers during the preparation process. An icon is included at the top of each recipe and designed to provide a quick visual cue for the type of cooking method required. The key to the icons is included in the table on the top of the next page.

Cooking equipment is listed for each recipe. In addition, there is a basic set of equipment assumed to be available in every Scout camp kitchen. This list of basics is covered in more detail in a following section.

## Recipe Icons Category System

| | |
|---|---|
| | Dutch oven with coals |
| | Cook pot on cookstove |
| | Frying pan on cookstove |
| | Foil, skewer, or other direct heating over coals or embers |
| | No heat source required |

## Challenge Level

Challenge level is indicated as easy, moderate, or difficult and, as previously discussed, given from the perspective of the young chef. The challenge level increases for recipes that call for more cooking steps, chopping, or attention to detail. Recipes considered difficult are purposely few in number

S'mores Dip is awesome! And it's all the better because, when it comes to cooking, it doesn't get much easier than this. *Christine Conners*

but are nevertheless provided to stretch the skills of young Scouts whom the adult in charge believes to be up to the test.

## Preparation Time

More hands make lighter work for many recipes, but not for all. *Scott Simerly*

Preparation time is estimated for two metrics: the total cooking time, from preparing the heat source all the way through to serving the food, and also for that portion of the cooking time relegated to the young Scouts assisting with the preparation. Not all Scouts will be able to maintain the same level of focus over equivalent time spans, and so this latter data is included to assist the adults with assignment of duties based on their good judgment. Note that cooking times assume food preparation occurring under pleasant weather conditions. Severe weather can be expected to significantly lengthen cooking times.

## Recommended Number of Chefs

Unique to this book is a recommendation on the number of chefs, both adults and young Scouts, for a given recipe. More challenging or multidimensional recipes can require more chefs in the process. And some recipes can benefit from having more than one Scout assisting, especially when chopping and mixing are involved. At the same time, this information is designed to prevent too many chefs in the kitchen, a common situation that can result in collisions and interference in confined areas and the distraction caused by that one kid with not enough to do.

## Preparation Instructions

The preparation steps form the core of each recipe, and these have also been given unique treatment in this book. When the chefs are young, not only is adult oversight required for every recipe, but most recipes require an adult to accomplish at least some of the steps, such as preparing the heat source. It is assumed that the adult in charge of overseeing meal preparation will assist the Scouts in gathering all necessary ingredients and equipment.

The preparation steps for the young Scouts are written using simpler and more descriptive language. The logic used to divide tasks between adults and kids was based on the level of complexity or risk associated with the preparation steps. Some recipes require an adult to both initiate and finish a recipe. But, to avoid defeating the purpose of this book, we did not include recipes that would require adults under normal circumstances to intervene repeatedly at other points in the preparation process. In practice, the actual dividing line between duties will depend on the Scout's basic motor skills and ability to focus and follow directions. In some situations, your young chefs may not be able to accomplish even the simplest tasks without assistance. To avoid injury and illness, continuous oversight, as well as good judgment in assigning cooking duties, must be exercised by the adult in charge.

## The Danger Zone

The cooking process is fraught with risks, both immediate (for example, cuts and burns) and longer term (food poisoning). The "Danger Zone" is a highlighted area, included with every recipe, that covers the key hazards associated with that recipe's preparation steps, such as sharp knives or hot and heavy cast iron. It is meant as a go-to source for the adult in charge to quickly review relevant safety hazards with the young chefs prior to commencement of cooking. These, of course, are not exhaustive lists and shouldn't be treated as such. However, with continuous exposure to a variety of safety topics, over time, the Scouts will begin to instinctually respect the hazards present in the kitchen and think with a mind more geared toward a reduction of risk.

## Contributor Information

Each recipe ends with biographical data on the Scout leader who provided the original information for that dish. Included are the leader's name, Scout affiliation, and hometown.

## Supplemental Information: The Appendices

The back matter in this book focuses on resources and references designed with both young chefs and adults in mind. Simple measurement conversions are covered in appendix A. Appendix B focuses on low-impact cooking and minimizing one's impact on the environment while camping. Finally, if you or your Scouts are interested in the fine art of baking in a box oven, find out how simple these are to construct in appendix C. Several recipes in this book can easily use a box oven instead of a Dutch oven.

This Girl Scout knows not to take chances when using hot coals with a Dutch oven. Barbecue gloves protect her hands and arms. *Allison Rudick*

# CAMP COOKING SAFETY

Removing ourselves from the insular bubble of everyday life is one of the great attractions of spending time in the outdoors for many people. Risk obviously comes with the territory. For Scouts in particular, being outdoors means being challenged in some fashion. And being challenged inherently implies being subjected to physical risk or emotional stress that one is not normally accustomed to. In a nutshell, we grow by placing ourselves in harm's way. In environments devoid of hazards, we stagnate.

There are countless creative ways to hurt oneself when camping. The risks are found around every corner. Tools, fire, wild animals, weather, poisonous plants and insects—these are just a few. But oftentimes the greatest hotbed of hazards on a camping trip is the one generally taken for granted: the camp kitchen.

Here, every time we camp, we have the very real potential of badly burning ourselves or the surrounding land, cutting our bodies, breaking our bones, instigating animal attacks, and poisoning ourselves and our fellow campers. Some of the hazards parallel those found in the home kitchen, but they are amplified in the outdoors while being compounded by many others that are unique to being outside. The danger of injury or illness while camping is further increased by what is typically the remote setting of the camp, far from doctor or hospital.

Even the best preparation and attention to detail can't guarantee that every trip will be free of accident or injury, but you can be sure that the outdoors does not long suffer the ill-prepared, careless, or foolhardy. The probability of harm and the severity of the hazards encountered can both be substantially reduced through the proper application of care and caution.

Review the key safety tips in this section, then summarize and share with your Scouts all applicable points prior to your next camping trip. Remember that no list can cover every danger lurking in a situation; but by becoming a lifelong student of safety, few situations will catch the chef ill-prepared or by surprise.

## Supervision

- Don't turn your young Scouts loose in the camp kitchen without expecting to devote constant adult oversight and guidance! As a general rule, the younger the Scout chef, the greater the level of adult supervision that will be required.

- Always have a first aid kit handy, one that at least meets the requirements established by your Scouting organization and contains the items necessary to treat common kitchen injuries such as cuts and burns.

- Chaos provides fertile ground for accident and injury. With that in mind, cooking with young, inexperienced Scouts should be conducted only after proper planning and preparation. The adult in charge should arrange the menu for the camping trip in advance and gather the necessary gear and ingredients so that all is ready for the kids once it's time to cook. Wait until the youngsters have a modest level of experience in the kitchen before attempting to engage them in "seat-of-the-pants" cooking activities.

When young kids cook, constant adult supervision is required, even when the Scouts are adept at using recipes designed for their age. *Scott Simerly*

## Camp Setup

- In the camp kitchen proper, place tables and cooking areas in a manner that supports unimpeded work flow. Avoid confined areas. It's particularly important to give young chefs plenty of elbow room, especially when more than one is using sharp utensils. For the same reason, keep the preparation area separated from the cooking zone to avoid collisions while chefs are working with or carrying scalding hot cookware.

- Set up the serving area on a table away from the kitchen to prohibit interference between chefs and diners. As serving time approaches, be especially vigilant at keeping hungry campers away from your young chefs while they focus on finishing their job.

- Give yourself and your young charges plenty of time to cook the meal. Never rush, even if you find yourselves falling behind. This is especially important when kids are cooking, because they generally lack the experience to safely pick up the tempo. Just let the schedule slip.

Keep the tents and high-traffic areas away from your camp kitchen. *Scott Simerly*

## Food Poisoning

- Most young chefs can readily understand why sharp knives and hot cookware can be hazardous, because they've experienced cuts and burns firsthand. Food poisoning, on the other hand, is a more esoteric problem, one for which it's harder for them to link cause and effect or to be convinced that it's a real hazard. This is a key reason why the dangers of food poisoning, and its prevention, should be taught at every opportunity, to remind youngsters that the threat is there. Specifically because young chefs often have yet to develop a full appreciation of the dangers posed by food that's been improperly stored or prepared, keen vigilance must be provided by the adult in charge to be certain that young Scouts follow strict rules of hygiene and sanitation while preparing food.

- Take a moment to explain to your young chefs the specific dangers posed by raw meat and eggs, how bacteria, viruses, and parasites are often found in these types of food, and how these microbes can cause a range of problems in people, from vomiting and diarrhea to, in some cases, death. Make it clear that this is why it's important for chefs to be very careful while working with food, to prevent people from becoming ill. Explain the main methods for preventing food-related sickness: 1) stopping the growth of harmful microbes through proper food storage, 2) avoiding the spread of harmful microbes through proper hygiene, and 3) eliminating any remaining microbes through proper food preparation. Each of these three topics is covered in more detail in the following points.

- Always cover foods to help keep invisible microbes from drifting onto it; a cover also blocks insects, such as flies, from spreading disease to your food. Store foods at close to freezing temperature to help prevent the growth of any microbes that may already be on your food. So keep foods and opened food containers properly sealed and on ice in a cooler until it's time to prepare the meal. Be sure to cover cooked foods at serving time. And place any leftovers in a sealed food-storage container on ice immediately following the meal.

- Before handling any food for the first time, all chefs should sanitize their hands with a thorough washing using soap and water followed by a complete drying. Once food preparation commences, hands should always be washed after handling raw meat or eggs but before touching anything else. If raw meat and eggs must be repeatedly touched during the cooking process, then hands should be repeatedly sanitized. Be compulsive about this! Hands that aren't sanitized can easily spread harmful microbes to other foods or serving utensils and eventually infect the hapless diners who aren't aware of the invisible danger.

- Some surfaces, such as mixing bowls, knives, and cutting boards, will become contaminated while working with raw meats and eggs before these ingredients are cooked. This is normal. However, it is essential to keep all contaminated utensils away from foods already cooked or those that will be served raw, such as salads and fresh fruits and vegetables. Transferral of harmful pathogens to such foods is called cross-contamination and is a common cause of food-related illness.

- It's natural to use cutting boards, mixing bowls, knives, and other utensils for more than one purpose in the kitchen, especially when multiple chefs are assisting. But it's easy to lose track of which utensils were previously used for what purpose. It's essential that young chefs be taught not to use kitchen tools without knowing for certain if there is a risk of cross-contamination. Even better, the chefs should each use their own dedicated equipment. In any case, teach your chefs to ask, and if they're still not certain, to rewash the gear before using it again.

- A chef who sustains a cut, no matter how minor, should immediately stop food preparation to avoid contaminating food with blood. If any food may have been contaminated by blood, it should be discarded. No chef with open wounds on hands or arms should participate in food preparation. While on this unpleasant subject, but in a similar vein, youngsters with runny noses should sit on the bench until feeling better.

- When storing food on ice, it's important to keep raw meat and eggs in a dedicated cooler. As ice melts, the cold water tends to eventually penetrate almost any packaging. Cross-contamination then ensures that whatever nasties may have been on the meat or eggs will be in the cold water as well. For this reason, any foods that won't eventually be cooked, such as raw vegetable and fruits, condiments in containers, or leftovers, should be kept in their own cooler. Bottled or canned beverages, drinking water, and drinking ice are best stored in a third cooler. Wrap a blanket or sleeping bag around your cooler to insulate it and to slow the melting of ice.

- All foods containing raw meats or eggs must be thoroughly cooked to a temperature high enough to ensure that any harmful microbes will perish. The optimum cooking temperature depends on the type of food being cooked. But when cooking with kids, it's best to keep it simple and set the target to at least 165 °F, the temperature that guarantees the elimination of all harmful food pathogens. Use a food thermometer with an easy-read dial or meter, and teach your young chefs to carefully take multiple temperature measurements, especially in thick cuts of meat. To keep the measurements from being biased, show them how to make measurements in the center of the cut, away from any bone.

- Water is an essential ingredient in many recipes, of course. Its purity is taken for granted in the home kitchen; and in many camping situations, safe drinking water is provided on-site. In some campgrounds, however, spigots can not be relied upon to provide safe water. An adult leader should take the time in advance to inquire about the quality of the water at the camp to be visited. If safe water may not be available, plan to bring plenty of potable water for drinking and cooking. One gallon per person per day in mild weather is a good rule of thumb.

## Cuts, Burns, and Broken Bones

- Knife blades pose one of the more obvious hazards in the camp kitchen. Proper blade maintenance and use are essential for avoiding injury. It's important to keep blade edges sharp, because a dull blade slips much more frequently during use and can more easily end up slicing your hand or fingers because of it. When using knives, teach Scouts to always keep their fingers away from the blade edge and tip and to avoid excessive, unnecessary movement of the knife. Learn how to chop with a chef's knife using a rocking motion of the blade on its forward edge, and instruct the Scouts how to do the same. The Whittling Chip, for Cub Scouts, and the Totin' Chip, for Boy Scouts, are awards earned for proper use of sharp instruments, including pocket knives. While geared more toward safety with woodworking tools, some leaders nevertheless require that Scouts earn the appropriate award before permitting them to use knives in the camp kitchen, because the training helps illustrate the dangers of any tool with sharp edges.

- Sharp knives should never be left in a bin of wash water with other dishes because they can remain hidden until some unlucky Scout reaches into the suds and receives a nasty cut. Teach your young Scouts to always leave knives where the blades can be seen; and, when washing, don't soak them along with the other dishes. When storing knives, it's a good idea to place each blade in its own protective cover. This not only helps to protect the blade from dulling but also prevents inadvertent cuts to the chefs reaching into a container or drawer for other tools and utensils.

- Hot surfaces are another obvious hazard found in the camp kitchen. These may be a just-used stove, a frying pan recently moved from the flames, a Dutch oven straight from the coals, baked potatoes wrapped in foil, or a pot of stew, to name a few. All are capable of producing severe scalds or burns. To reduce the risk, always place hot items in a safe location away from foot traffic and keep constant mental note of where they are. Warn fellow chefs and campers of any particular danger. And, by all means, always wear protective barbecue gloves or use pads when moving hot items.

- While working with pots and pans on a cookstove  or when moving these items to a serving area, be sure to keep long pot or pan handles turned away from the edge of the table. Injuries are common where chefs snag a pot or pan handle and the scalding contents tumble onto their legs and feet.

- Pots or pans too large for the young chef to handle safely or with bases too big for the cookstove are another potential hazard because of the risk of either dropping the cookware or having it inadvertently slide to the ground. Scalding and broken bones are the dangers here. If the cookware is heavy, insist that your Scouts ask for help when moving it. If the pot or pan is too large and unstable for your stove, then cook using gear that is better matched.

- A flimsy table is prone to collapse, and all the wobbling can send gear and food crashing to the ground. In the camp kitchen, this is a disaster waiting to happen. When cooking or serving, never use a table that lacks good stability and rigidity.

- In addition to unfailing use of barbecue gloves and hot pads, always wear closed-toe shoes when cooking and, preferably, long pants. Closed-toe shoes help protect feet from heavy or hot items accidently dropped on the ground, such as cast iron cookware or charcoal briquettes. And long pants can help prevent burns from hot foods inadvertently sloshed from pan or pot. This is a particularly important point to make with young Scouts, who may be more inclined to wear sandals or shorts but who are also more likely to lack the strength and motor skills to always keep hot food and gear where it belongs.

## Fire

- Perform all cooking in a fire-safe area of camp, clear of natural material that burns, such as dry leaves, grass, and overhanging shrubs and trees. Cook well away from any wooden structures. When cooking directly on the ground using coals, be sure that the cooking area is covered in a durable, fireproof material such as rock, gravel, or bare earth. Be sure to follow any special fire restrictions established for your region. Ask camp officials about this when checking in. Always have a large bucket of water handy to rapidly douse any flames that may escape your fire-safe perimeter.

- When cooking with a wood fire, don't make the fire larger than necessary for the cooking job. If the fire is too large, it will be difficult, if not impossible, to control the cooking process. It's also much easier to suffer burns from a large fire, especially when reaching in to place or move food items. Wood fire cooking is best performed over a bed of embers and ash, once the wood has been mostly consumed, because the heat is more predictable, uniform, and easier to control. More important, ember cooking provides a safer cooking environment, especially for young Scouts, because the flames are lower. So if the fire is too large, give it time to settle down before cooking. And be sure that the chefs always use long-sleeved barbecue gloves and long-handled tongs when managing foods in a wood fire.

- Hot coals on the ground can pose a hazard long after cooking is over. Dispose of spent coals in the fire pit or a fire-safe area well away from foot traffic. If this isn't possible, notify Scouts and Scouters of the danger of hot coals on the ground, and keep the area off limits to all but essential personnel until the coals expire.

- Never cook in a closed-wall tent, because noxious fumes will be trapped and can cause illness or death to those inside. A closed tent also poses a serious entrapment hazard should it catch fire. A kitchen tent or tarp structure must have all sides open to permit full ventilation and easy escape should the

This young Scout may look apprehensive, but he has little to fear with the wood fire well contained in a fire-safe area. *Scott Simerly*

need arise. The peak of a kitchen tent must also be significantly higher than the head of the tallest occupant so that any trapped fumes won't pose a breathing hazard. Never use a barbecue grill or wood fire under a kitchen tent! Flare-up creates a fire hazard, and excessive smoke can overwhelm even the best ventilation.

## Food Allergies and Intolerance

The way to deal with food allergies and food intolerance is to consider them during the planning process, not once you get to camp. Ask Scouts and Scouters if any have issues with certain kinds of food before the recipes are selected and the groceries bought.

## Wild Animals

Animals searching for food scraps and garbage can pose a danger to the camp environment either through aggression or disease. Dirty dishes, unsecured garbage, food and coolers left in the open—these will eventually attract animal attention. Wildlife that gains access to such goodies will surely come back for more, increasing the probability that people (and animals) will eventually suffer harm in the process. A camp that is kept neat and clean, with food and garbage securely stored, is far less attractive to the local fauna. Teach your Scouts to use low-impact camping principles and adhere to any food storage regulations unique to your area or camp.

# BASIC SKILLS

It goes without saying that young kids generally lack a grounding in the fundamentals of cooking. And why wouldn't they? They simply haven't had the time or, for many, the maturity to develop an impressive skill set in cookery. All too often nowadays, kids grow into adulthood lacking even the most rudimentary of culinary competence. So now is the time to begin teaching. As the young ones grow in confidence and capability, not only will they require less oversight and instruction, but they'll also become more adept at teaching themselves and others new techniques. Time taken now is an investment that will soon pay off in both the camp and home kitchens.

This section emphasizes fundamental skills that any new cook should understand and learn. The information is grouped topically around specific tips and methods and is presented from the vantage of the young. It is not a comprehensive list that an adult or older Scout might be expected to become familiar with. It is assumed that the material will be taught and demonstrated to the young Scouts by an adult.

The recipes in this book are mostly self-contained in the sense that relevant safety information is included in each recipe and the preparation steps are written assuming that the Scouts have no preexisting skill in the kitchen. But that doesn't mean there isn't anything to be gained through additional instruction, of course. With a broader understanding of cooking in general, young cooks will be able to reason through more questions themselves regarding recipes and, more important, avoid accident or injury in the kitchen.

Take time to teach these points to your Scouts, perhaps a few at a time, and especially those most relevant to any upcoming camping expedition. A thorough grounding in basic skills must also include a heavy emphasis on safety. In fact, the two are inseparable. So don't neglect the teaching of the safety-related topics found in the previous section.

## Plan in Advance

- Ask your young Scouts to help with selecting recipes for your upcoming camping trip. Not only will they be excited once the time comes for them to help create a meal they've helped plan, but they will also be less likely to grumble about food they've had a role in preparing.

- When selecting recipes, match their challenge level to the experience and maturity level of the young Scouts who will be doing the cooking. Keep this in mind once at camp when assigning Scouts to cooking duty. Assigning recipes that exceed the skill level of the cooks is a sure path to discouragement, not only for them, but for the adults who are charged with overseeing their work.

- Keep in mind the weather forecast when planning your menu for the upcoming camping trip. Some types of cooking will be inappropriate for young Scouts to attempt in poor weather. If the forecast is dicey, plan a simple menu built around cooking methods that are flexible for your situation. An example might be using a cookstove under a kitchen tarp.

## Know Your Recipes and Gear

- Before preparing a recipe, read through the instructions and be sure you have all the gear and ingredients necessary to do the job. It's frustrating to get halfway through the preparation only to learn that you don't understand the directions or don't have the equipment or ingredients to finish the meal.

- If you are using cooking gear for the first time, ask how to properly operate it. This is especially important when using stoves, sharp cooking instruments, or complicated gear. Don't simply assume that you know how. Much equipment has been damaged and many people injured because chefs didn't ask questions when they should have.

- Learn to recognize the difference in measuring sizes, especially between a teaspoon and a tablespoon. This is especially important when it comes to measuring salt, herbs, and spices. Be certain that all chefs know how to work with fractions.

- Never delay in seeking help if you think you need it. If you aren't sure that you understand a recipe's instructions, find someone competent to explain them. If a recipe or cooking task seems too difficult, ask for assistance.

## Be Healthy and Creative

- At times, you'll be tasked with preparing a recipe that someone else has chosen for you. Other times, you will be the one who is asked to select the recipes for a meal. When the choice is yours, always think about healthy options. Avoid choosing fatty or sugary recipes for every part of the meal. Instead, if you've selected a rich main course, then pair it with a healthy side dish or salad. Likewise, if a sumptuous dessert is on the menu, then choose a healthier option for your main course. On the same thought, if a heavy breakfast, lunch, or dinner is planned, lighten up on the other meals that day to give everyone's body a break.

- When you're in charge of the menu, skip the soda and sugary beverages at the main meals. They aren't good for your body. Instead, drink water or pure fruit juices, and be content, instead, with desserts or snacks for satisfying that sweet tooth.

Teach your young Scouts to use healthy dishes, such as the Chicken Caesar Salad shown here, to balance less healthy parts of the meal, such as a heavy dessert. *Christine Conners*

- Don't be afraid to try herbs and spices! They are what turn many otherwise bland foods into the things we love. A recipe will often tell you exactly which flavorings to use and how much. Other times, a recipe may say to use them "to taste," meaning to your individual preference.

## Control the Heat

- One of the most common problems new cooks face is burning food. Whether in a pot over the stove, on a barbecue grill, or in a foil pack in the fire, every chef has burned a lot of meals along the way. Unfortunately, it's easy to do. But, on the flip side, it's almost as easy to avoid. The secret is twofold: First, control the flame. Start with less heat, then increase it once you're sure you can avoid burning the food. Second, occasionally move the food to avoid dwelling too long in hot spots. This means stirring food in a pot, moving meat on the grill, rotating the Dutch oven over the coals, or turning or repositioning foil packs in the fire.

- Don't try to grill foods, bake foil packs, or cook marshmallows or breads-on-a-stick over a raging wood fire. If you do, scorched food is guaranteed. It's best to let the flames die down, then cook over the embers that remain. This will still give plenty of heat to do the work, and it will be distributed more uniformly, making it easier to cook food without charring some and undercooking the rest.

- Even when cooking on a bed of embers, foil packets are always challenging, because you can't see the food while it's cooking. As a result, it's easier to undercook or burn your food. The best way to cook in foil is to start with good recipes and then learn from experience. But a couple of tips will get you started: First, to help ensure that the food in your foil cooks evenly, seal the pack very tightly to trap in steam. Second, to avoid burning meat, set it on a bed of thinly sliced tomatoes, onions, or cabbage leaves before wrapping in foil. Be sure that the side of the foil pack set on the embers is the one containing the vegetables. The veggies may char, but their job is to release moisture and help insulate the rest of the food from extreme heat while it cooks.

- When using a pan for frying or for making pancakes, be prepared to lower the flame as you cook more batches of food. The pan will become hotter with time, and you'll find that it becomes easier to burn foods unless the flame is reduced. Also rotate foods out of the center of the frying pan, which tends to be the hottest area when the pan is used over a cookstove.

If you can cook perfect pancakes, you're well on your way to becoming a master of heat control, like this young Scout. *Scott Simerly*

- It's surprisingly difficult to burn many foods in a Dutch oven, even if you don't follow an exact coal count. This is especially true if you follow a few simple rules: Don't let the coals underneath the oven touch the metal; don't allow food in the oven to touch the inside of the lid if coals are used on the lid; keep coals evenly distributed (that is, don't let them clump up); rotate the lid and the base about a quarter-turn every 15 minutes or so; and pay close attention to time, especially when baking. Together, all these tips are very effective at preventing hot spots from forming in the metal, so food is less likely to burn.

- Food will occasionally undercook when using a Dutch oven. To be sure that more of the heat stays where it belongs to help the food cook properly, don't take the lid off unless you must. Don't cook over coals that have been placed on bare soil (moisture in the dirt can cause the coals to extinguish; use a metal tray or foil for your coals instead). Finally, when cooking for a long period of time, be sure to refresh your coals before they turn completely to ash, every 45 to 60 minutes.

## Deal with the Weather

- Windy weather presents a challenge for any type of cooking, because it's more difficult to control heat in the wind. Cooking behind a windbreak helps. Be especially careful when removing the lid from a Dutch oven in windy weather if coals are on the lid. Move the lid immediately downwind; otherwise, ash that blows off the lid could land in your food.

- Immediately ask for assistance if the weather begins to turn foul, with rain, snow, high wind, or lightning. At the least, you'll want to finish the cooking tasks as quickly and safely as you can. In severe weather, your goal should be to secure the camp kitchen and move to safe shelter as soon as possible. The cooking can wait until the threat has passed.

## Reduce, Reuse, and Recycle

- A group of Scouts will create a lot of trash over a camping weekend when using disposable servingware: paper plates, Styrofoam cups, plastic knives and spoons, and so on. Reduce your environmental footprint by asking the campers to bring their own personal mess kits from home: serving plate, bowl, cup, and cutlery. Sure, it will create extra work when it comes time to wash the dishes, but there will be a lot less waste to haul out once you leave.

- Don't forget to gather up all empty plastic, glass, and metal food and beverage containers so that they can be recycled.

## Clean Up

- Use at least two large basins when washing the cooking gear, dishes, and cutlery: one for the soapy water, the other for clean water for rinsing. Be sure to have plenty of scrub pads and drying towels so that several people can help at the same time.

- For cookware and dishes that are greasy, warm water cuts fats and oils much better than cold. Heat a pot of water over the stove or fire during dinner, then carefully pour it into a washbasin partly filled with unheated water. Be sure to get help pouring if the pot is too heavy, and don't make the wash water too hot to comfortably use.

- When washing dishes, use just enough detergent to do the job and no more. Too much isn't good for the environment, and it can be tough to thoroughly rinse from the dishes.

- Dump used wash water in "gray water" disposal pits, if these are provided in camp. If disposal pits are not provided, pick out any large bits of food from the wash water, then spread the water over a large area of ground away from the main camp. Never pour waste water into or near a lake or stream.

A happy attitude helps to make a humdrum chore go by faster. This young Scout is putting the principle into action! *Scott Simerly*

## Take Special Care of Cast Iron

Cast iron cookware is very durable, but it needs some special treatment to keep it in good shape. Following these simple steps, your cast iron can easily last a century or more.

- Never use a metal scrub pad when cleaning cast iron. It will destroy the natural black protective coating, known as patina. The patina not only keeps rust from forming but also keeps food from sticking. Use plastic scrub pads and scrapers instead. If tough, stuck-on food remains, pour warm water into the cookware and let soak for about 15 minutes before scrubbing again.

- Use wooden or plastic utensils when cooking with cast iron, and avoid metal utensils for the same reason that you avoid a metallic scrub pad: metal utensils can damage the patina.

- It may sound wacky, but don't use detergent on cast iron unless absolutely necessary to cut grease. Even then, use as little as possible, because it can harm the patina. A better option is to cut the grease using warm water.

- After you've cleaned and dried your cast iron, pour a little vegetable oil or food-grade mineral oil into the skillet or oven and wipe it around using a pad or paper towel. Make sure to thoroughly cover all surfaces, inside and out. Don't use so much oil that it pools up. If your cookware has been stored for more than a few days, when it comes time to cook, spread a thin layer of oil inside the skillet or oven before using. Oiling your cookware after washing keeps it from rusting, and oiling it immediately before cooking helps to strengthen the patina.

Cast iron makes for wonderful camp cookware, but it requires a little special treatment to ensure that it will last a century or more. *Christine Conners*

# BASIC EQUIPMENT

A lot of equipment isn't needed to be a successful camp chef. In fact, even less is needed when cooking with young Scouts, because the emphasis should be on building a foundation in the basics, not on less-used techniques that often require more gear. To help match recipes to your available gear, the recipes in this book are subdivided based on cooking method so that if, say, you have no Dutch oven, you'll be able to focus on other options.

Space doesn't permit a comprehensive discussion of all cooking gear options, which, these days, seem to be nearly endless. Instead, what follows is a listing in general terms of essential equipment that all chefs should have handy at camp. Also covered is a listing of key gear necessary for each of the primary cooking methods typically used when camping.

Recipes occasionally call for items that are required for that recipe's preparation but might otherwise be considered nonessential in a collection of standard kitchen gear. Such items aren't listed here but are instead included in the recipe's required equipment list.

## Essential Equipment:

- 3 coolers, one for raw meats and eggs, the second for other food items, the third for beverages and drinking ice
- Sturdy folding tables
- An assortment of measuring cups and spoons
- 2 chef's knives, with sheaths or container
- 2 paring knives, with sheaths or container
- 2 cutting boards
- Can opener
- Bowls—an assortment of small, medium, and large sizes
- Long-handled wooden spoon

- Long-handled spatula (for flipping pancakes, eggs, etc.)
- Long-handled serving ladle
- Long-handled tongs
- Food thermometer
- Hand sanitizer
- Paper towels
- Cooking spray or vegetable oil, for greasing frying pans and Dutch ovens
- Heavy-duty aluminum foil
- Servingware (dishes, bowls, cups, and cutlery) appropriate for the group size, if campers do not have personal mess kits
- Paper napkins
- Ziplock freezer bags, quart and gallon sizes
- 2 washbasins
- 2 nonmetallic scrub pads
- Dish detergent
- Plenty of dish towels
- Heavy-duty trash bags
- Heavy barbecue gloves
- 2 or more long-neck lighters
- Bins of appropriate size for storing kitchen gear

## Nonessential but Valuable Auxiliary Equipment:

- Serving table, if picnic table or the like is not available at camp
- Kitchen tarp and associated poles and rope
- Spice and herb kit

## For Cooking with Coals:

- 12-inch/6-quart-capacity camp Dutch oven, the most common oven size found in Scouting. A range of oven sizes gives the chef a lot of flexibility, but for this book the 12-inch oven is large enough for all recipes.
- Briquettes, of good quality and of standard size, important when using a recipe book such as this one which specifies exact coal counts
- Charcoal starter and newspaper, if lighter fluid isn't used
- Metallic coal tray, such as a pizza pan
- Long-handled tongs, for handling the coals
- Lid lifter, a metal device for securely lifting a hot oven lid
- Trivet, a three-point device on which a pan rests inside a Dutch oven

## For Cooking over a Burner:

- Camp stove, large enough to handle your pots and pans
- Fuel appropriate for your camp stove
- Cooking pots—an assortment of small, medium, and large sizes
- Frying pan, preferably two sizes, one medium-size, the other larger

## For Cooking over a Wood Fire:

- Firewood and fire starting material
- Sturdy portable grill stand, if no grill grate is built into the fire ring
- Long-handled camping forks

Always review with your young Scouts the equipment required for the form of cooking you'll be using on the next trip. *Tim Conners*

# Camper's Caramel Biscuits

**REQUIRED EQUIPMENT:**
12-inch camp Dutch oven with trivet
Briquettes and accessories for Dutch oven
9-inch pie pan

**INITIAL PREPARATION STEP FOR ADULTS:**
Prepare 25 briquettes for the Dutch oven.

**PREPARATION STEPS FOR YOUNG SCOUTS:**
1. Cover the inside of a round baking pan with cooking spray. Do this while an adult prepares the coals for the Dutch oven.

2. Open the container of biscuit dough by whomping it on the side of something hard, like a picnic table. With clean hands, remove the dough and pull it apart into eight dough disks.

3. Break each dough disk into four pieces.

4. Set all the dough pieces in the bottom of the pan.

5. Drizzle the caramel topping over the dough, then sprinkle the chopped pecans over the topping.

6. Set the pan in the Dutch oven on a trivet. If you don't know what a trivet is, see Chef's Corner.

7. Once the adult says the coals are ready, put the lid on the oven, then set the oven on a metal tray. Place 17 coals on the lid and 8 coals underneath the oven.

8. Check the biscuits after about 25 minutes. They are ready to serve once the biscuit dough has risen and the top of the bread has become a golden brown color.

**FINAL PREPARATION STEP FOR ADULTS:**
Assist the Scouts with removing the pan of bread from the hot oven.

**Allison Rudick, Trussville, Alabama**
Leader
Troop 872, Girl Scouts of
North-Central Alabama

**INGREDIENTS**
Cooking spray

1 (16.3-ounce) container Pillsbury Original Home-style Grands! refrigerated biscuits

½ cup Smucker's hot caramel topping

½ cup chopped pecans

### DANGER ZONE:

- Hot coals! Enforce your fire-safe zone and use your gloves.

- Hot and heavy cookware! Use your gloves.

### Chef's Corner
A *trivet* is a small metal plate with three short legs. It's used to keep pies and cakes from burning by lifting them above the hot floor of a Dutch oven. A substitute can be made using three small rocks or wads of foil.

Servings: 4 to 6
Preparation Time—Total: 45 minutes
Preparation Time—For the Scouts: 45 minutes
Recommended Number of Chefs: 1 Scout and 1 adult
Challenge Level: Easy

# Quirky Quiche

## INGREDIENTS

2 green onions

1 (7-ounce) can Spam

4 eggs

1 cup milk

1 cup shredded cheddar cheese

1 (9-inch) deep-dish frozen pie crust, in pan

## REQUIRED EQUIPMENT:

12-inch camp Dutch oven with trivet
Briquettes and accessories for Dutch oven
Chef's knife
Large mixing bowl
Wooden spoon

## INITIAL PREPARATION STEPS FOR ADULTS:

1. Remove premade pie crust from cooler.

2. Prepare 29 briquettes for the Dutch oven, then preheat oven using 10 coals on a metal tray underneath and 19 coals on the lid.

## PREPARATION STEPS FOR YOUNG SCOUTS:

1. Cut the ragged top parts from the green onions and throw the ragged pieces away. Remove the stringy roots too. Chop the rest of the green onions into pieces. Do this while an adult prepares the Dutch oven.

2. Open the can of Spam and drain the liquid into the trash. Remove the Spam from the can, then chop the meat into small cubes. The cubes should be a little smaller than the size of dice.

3. Crack the eggs into a large bowl.

4. To the bowl with the eggs, add the milk, the shredded cheddar cheese, the chopped green onions, and the chopped Spam. Stir all the ingredients together with a wooden spoon.

5. Carefully pour the mixture containing the eggs and Spam into the pie crust shell.

Servings: 6 to 8
Preparation Time—Total: 1 hour
Preparation Time—For the Scouts: 15 minutes
Recommended Number of Chefs: 2 Scouts and 1 adult
Challenge Level: Moderate

## FINAL PREPARATION STEPS FOR ADULTS:

1. Remove hot lid from the Dutch oven and carefully set the filled pie pan on a trivet in the oven.

2. Replace lid, ensuring an even distribution of 19 coals on the lid and 10 under the oven.

3. Bake for about 30 minutes, until eggs have become firm.

4. Remove pie pan from the oven and allow quiche to cool for about 10 minutes before serving.

**Tim and Christine Conners, Statesboro, Georgia**
Committee Members and Merit Badge Counselors
Troop 340, Coastal Empire Council

### Chef's Corner
Learning how to successfully crack an egg takes practice. The easiest way is to hit the side of the egg against a hard object using just enough force to put a crack in it, not smash it. Then use your thumb tips to separate the shell along the crack.

Don't let the name fool you. The only thing quirky about this quiche is how delicious it is! *Christine Conners*

**HOT TIP!**
Don't trim too much from the onions, or you won't have much left over for the recipe.

## INGREDIENTS

Cooking spray

3 cups Krusteaz butter-milk pancake mix

2 cups water

10 fully cooked sausage links

Maple syrup to taste

# Flying Saucer Sausage Pancakes

"We wanted a no-fuss way of preparing pancakes and sausage for several people, and this recipe is the result. Cooking and cleanup are much easier by doing it all with one oven. The fact that it looks like a flying saucer is just a bonus!"

### REQUIRED EQUIPMENT:
12-inch camp Dutch oven
Briquettes and accessories for Dutch oven
Heavy-duty aluminum foil
Large mixing bowl
Wooden spoon
Spatula

### INITIAL PREPARATION STEP FOR ADULTS:
Prepare 25 briquettes for the Dutch oven.

### PREPARATION STEPS FOR YOUNG SCOUTS:

1. Cover the inside of the Dutch oven with aluminum foil. Press it tightly against the bottom and wall, then spray the foil with cooking spray. Do this while an adult prepares the coals for the oven.

2. Dump the pancake mix into a large bowl, then add the 2 cups of water to the bowl.

3. Stir the pancake mix with a wooden spoon until the batter becomes smooth with no large lumps remaining in it.

4. Pour the pancake batter into the Dutch oven.

5. Gently set the sausage links on top of the pancake batter. Arrange the sausage links like spokes on a bicycle wheel. Don't push the links down into the batter!

Servings: 10
Preparation Time—Total: 1 hour
Preparation Time—For the Scouts: 1 hour
Recommended Number of Chefs: 2 Scouts and 1 adult
Challenge Level: Easy

6. Once the adult says the coals are ready, put the lid on the oven, then set the oven on a metal tray. Place 8 coals under the oven and 17 coals on the lid.

7. Bake for 30 to 35 minutes.

## FINAL PREPARATION STEPS FOR ADULTS:

1. Move the pancake from the Dutch oven and remove the foil.

2. Slice the "pancake" into ten wedges using a knife or the edge of a spatula. Make sure there is a sausage in every wedge.

3. Serve with maple syrup to taste.

**Allison Rudick, Trussville, Alabama**
Leader
Troop 872, Girl Scouts of North-Central Alabama

HOT TIP!
Be certain that only fully cooked sausage is used in this recipe!

**DANGER ZONE:**

• Hot coals! Enforce your fire-safe zone and use your gloves.

• Hot and heavy cookware! Use your gloves.

Okay, so maybe it looks more like a wagon wheel than a flying saucer, but it's still easy and awesome. *Christine Conners*

## Alex's Eggstra Good Breakfast

### INGREDIENTS
Cooking spray

8 slices bread

1 (16-ounce) carton Original Egg Beaters

1½ cups milk

½ teaspoon salt

6 ounces cooked ham or cooked sausage

2 cups grated cheese, your choice

Optional: maple syrup

### REQUIRED EQUIPMENT:
12-inch camp Dutch oven
Briquettes and accessories for Dutch oven
Medium-size mixing bowl
Wooden spoon
Chef's knife

### INITIAL PREPARATION STEPS FOR ADULTS:
1. Prepare 25 briquettes for the Dutch oven.

2. About 45 minutes after starting the first batch of coals, begin a second batch of 25.

### PREPARATION STEPS FOR YOUNG SCOUTS:
1. Spray the inside of the Dutch oven with cooking spray. Do this while an adult prepares the coals for the Dutch oven.

2. Tear the slices of bread into small pieces. Place the bread pieces in the Dutch oven.

3. Pour the Egg Beaters into a medium-size bowl along with the milk.

4. Add the salt to the bowl. Stir well with a wooden spoon.

5. Pour the egg mixture over the bread pieces in the Dutch oven. Be sure to cover all the bread.

6. Slice the ham or sausage into small pieces using a chef's knife, then place the pieces of meat over the bread in the oven. You'll need about 6 ounces of meat for this step. Ask an adult for help if you're not sure how much meat you have available.

7. Sprinkle the grated cheese over the bread and meat in the oven.

Servings: 8 to 10
Preparation Time—Total: 1 hour and 15 minutes
Preparation Time—For the Scouts: 30 minutes
Recommended Number of Chefs: 2 Scouts and 1 adult
Challenge Level: Moderate

8. Once the adult says the coals are ready, put the lid on the oven, then set the oven on a metal tray. Place 8 coals under the oven and 17 coals on the lid.

## FINAL PREPARATION STEPS FOR ADULTS:

1. Take over the preparation from the Scouts, cooking the egg dish for about an hour, until the cheese is melted and the dish becomes firm. Note that the coals will need to be refreshed about 45 minutes after the lid goes on the oven.

2. Serve with optional maple syrup.

**Allison Rudick, Trussville, Alabama**
Leader
Troop 872, Girl Scouts of North-Central Alabama

**DANGER ZONE:**

- Hot coals! Enforce your fire-safe zone and use your gloves.
- Sharp utensils! Careful slicing required.
- Hot and heavy cookware! Use your gloves.

## Peter Piper's Pancake Puddin'

Peter Piper prepped a pot of pancake puddin'.
A pot of pancake puddin' Peter Piper prepped.
If Peter Piper prepped a pot of pancake puddin',
Where's the pot of pancake puddin' Peter Piper
    prepped?

**INGREDIENTS**

3 eggs

½ cup granulated sugar

1 teaspoon salt

4 cups milk

2 cups all-purpose flour

½ cup (1 standard stick) butter

Maple syrup to taste

**REQUIRED EQUIPMENT:**
12-inch camp Dutch oven
Briquettes and accessories for Dutch oven
Large mixing bowl
Wooden spoon

**INITIAL PREPARATION STEPS FOR ADULTS:**

1. Prepare 29 briquettes for the Dutch oven.

2. Warm the oven over 10 coals on a metal tray.

**PREPARATION STEPS FOR YOUNG SCOUTS:**

1. Crack the eggs into a large bowl, then mix them by stirring very quickly with a fork. Do this while an adult prepares the Dutch oven.

2. Add the sugar, salt, milk, and flour to the large bowl with the eggs in it. Mix everything with a large wooden spoon until there are no more large lumps left in the batter.

3. Once the adult says the Dutch oven is ready to use, melt the stick of butter in the oven.

4. Pour the batter from the large bowl into the Dutch oven over the melted butter. Don't stir the batter with the butter!

5. Set the lid on the Dutch oven.

6. Place 19 coals on the lid, leaving 10 coals under the oven.

**HOT TIP!**
If you accidentally crack large pieces of shell into the bowl, pick them out with clean fingers; but then sanitize your hands before touching anything else!

Servings: 10 to 12
Preparation Time—Total: 1 hour and 15 minutes
Preparation Time—For the Scouts: 30 minutes
Recommended Number of Chefs: 2 Scouts and 1 adult
Challenge Level: Moderate

## FINAL PREPARATION STEPS FOR ADULTS:

1. Bake for about 50 minutes, until the crust has risen and turned a golden brown. Use a few more briquettes if the coals have mostly eroded to ash.

2. Serve with maple syrup.

**Carl Laub, Arlington Heights, Illinois**
Executive Board Member
Northwest Suburban Council

**Chef's Corner**
The clear stuff from a raw egg is really hard to mix with the yellow yolk. Try doing it with a spoon, and you'll see why a fork works better!

No, it isn't pizza. It's a pancake! *Christine Conners*

**DANGER ZONE:**

• Hot coals! Enforce your fire-safe zone and use your gloves.

• Raw eggs! Sanitize your hands after handling.

• Hot and heavy cookware! Use your gloves.

## Widdle Waddle Waffle Breakfast

**INGREDIENTS**

1 dozen eggs

1 cup milk

1 cup maple syrup

½ teaspoon salt

1 pound maple pork sausage

10 premade frozen waffles

### REQUIRED EQUIPMENT:
12-inch camp Dutch oven
Briquettes and accessories for Dutch oven
Large mixing bowl
Wooden spoon
Spatula

### INITIAL PREPARATION STEPS FOR ADULTS:
1. Prepare 25 briquettes for the Dutch oven, then preheat oven for about 10 minutes using all the coals on a metal tray underneath the oven.

2. About 45 minutes after starting the first batch of coals, begin a second batch of 25.

### PREPARATION STEPS FOR YOUNG SCOUTS:
1. Crack the eggs into a large bowl, then add the milk to the bowl. Do this while an adult prepares the Dutch oven.

2. Pour the maple syrup into the bowl with the eggs, then add the salt. Mix everything well with a wooden spoon.

3. Once the adult says the oven is ready, add the maple pork sausage to the oven. Fry the sausage while breaking up the large lumps with the wooden spoon. Cook the sausage until no pink remains in the meat, but don't burn it.

4. Tear the waffles into large pieces and lay the pieces over the hot sausage in the oven.

5. Pour the egg mixture over the waffles and sausage.

6. Place the lid on the Dutch oven, then move 17 of the coals from under the oven to the lid. Make sure the coals are evenly spread on the lid and underneath.

Servings: 10 to 12
Preparation Time—Total: 1 hour and 30 minutes
Preparation Time—For the Scouts: 30 minutes
Recommended Number of Chefs: 2 Scouts and 1 adult
Challenge Level: Moderate

**FINAL PREPARATION STEPS FOR ADULTS:**

1. Take over the cooking from the Scouts after they move the coals into place.

2. Cook for 50 to 60 minutes until the eggs are no longer runny. The coals will need to be refreshed about 30 minutes after the Scouts put the lid on.

3. Remove the oven from the coals, slice the waffle cake like a pizza, then serve with a spatula.

**Tim and Christine Conners, Statesboro, Georgia**
Committee Members and Merit Badge Counselors
Troop 340, Coastal Empire Council

**DANGER ZONE:**

- Hot coals! Enforce your fire-safe zone and use your gloves.

- Raw eggs! Sanitize your hands after handling.

- Hot and heavy cookware! Use your gloves.

# Eagle River Sausage Burritos

## INGREDIENTS

1 pound precooked frozen sausage patties

Cooking spray

6 eggs

6 (8-inch) flour tortillas

1 (16-ounce) jar salsa

## REQUIRED EQUIPMENT:

Cookstove
Medium-size frying pan
Wooden spoon

## INITIAL PREPARATION STEPS FOR ADULTS:

1. Precooked sausage patties come in a variety of types and sizes. The number of patties isn't important for this recipe, but the weight is. Set aside about 1 pound of patties for the Scouts if the package contains more than this amount.

2. The sausage must be thawed. If the patties have been in a cooler overnight, they shouldn't need more than about 30 to 60 minutes to soften unless the morning temperature is cold. If the patties are frozen or the air temperature cold, seal them in a ziplock bag and set the bag in warm water for about 15 minutes.

3. Prepare cookstove for the Scouts.

## PREPARATION STEPS FOR YOUNG SCOUTS:

1. Spray the inside of a medium-size frying pan with cooking spray.

2. Crumble the sausage patties into the pan. The pieces of sausage should be bite-size, not too large.

3. Crack the eggs over the sausage.

4. Place the frying pan on the stove over a flame that's halfway between the lowest and highest setting.

5. Stir the sausage and eggs together using a wooden spoon. Keep stirring while the eggs cook, to keep the food from burning.

6. Turn the heat off once the eggs are ready. The eggs are fully cooked when there is no clear, runny liquid remaining and they are yellow throughout.

Servings: 6
Preparation Time—Total: 30 minutes
Preparation Time—For the Scouts: 30 minutes
Recommended Number of Chefs: 2 Scouts and 1 adult
Challenge Level: Moderate

7. Lay a tortilla flat on a serving plate. Scoop some of the sausage-egg mixture onto the tortilla. You'll need enough of the sausage-egg mixture for six tortillas, so try not to use too much or too little.

8. Top the sausage and eggs with a couple of tablespoons of salsa, then roll the tortilla like you would a burrito by tucking the sides in, then rolling like a carpet. Ask an adult for help if you're having trouble with this step.

9. Repeat the laying out, filling, and rolling for the remaining five tortillas.

**Scott Simerly, Apex, North Carolina**
Senior Assistant Scoutmaster
Troop 204, Occoneechee Council

**DANGER ZONE:**

• Raw eggs! Sanitize your hands after handling.

• Hot and heavy cookware! Keep frying pan handle turned inward.

# Green Eggs and Ham

"Humans have five senses: sight, hearing, smell, taste, and touch. The sense of sight is one of our most powerful. Even though the color of food may not have anything to do with how it tastes, we tend to not eat something that doesn't look the way we're used to. In fact, you may be convinced food tastes bad, even when it's actually really good, just by how it looks. This recipe is a fun take on the famous story by Dr. Seuss and is a case in point. Try serving the first bite of Green Eggs and Ham to someone who has their eyes closed, then see what they say once they open their eyes!"

## INGREDIENTS

1 pound precooked ham

1 dozen eggs

1 cup milk

½ teaspoon salt

½ teaspoon ground black pepper

1 cup shredded cheese, your choice

¼ teaspoon green food coloring

2 tablespoons butter

## REQUIRED EQUIPMENT:

Cookstove
Chef's knife
Large mixing bowl
Wooden spoon
Large frying pan

## INITIAL PREPARATION STEP FOR ADULTS:

Prepare cookstove for the Scouts.

## PREPARATION STEPS FOR YOUNG SCOUTS:

1. Chop the ham into very small pieces using a chef's knife. Place the chopped ham in a large mixing bowl.

2. Crack the eggs into the bowl with the ham, then pour in the milk.

3. Add the salt and pepper to the bowl, followed by the shredded cheese.

4. Now comes the fun part: add the green food coloring to the bowl. Stir everything well with a wooden spoon until the eggs are fully mixed.

Servings: 8 to 10
Preparation Time—Total: 30 minutes
Preparation Time—For the Scouts: 30 minutes
Recommended Number of Chefs: 2 Scouts and 1 adult
Challenge Level: Moderate

5. Place a large frying pan on the stove and set the heat to medium, halfway between the lowest and highest settings.

6. Melt the butter in the pan, then spread the butter around to coat all the inside of the pan.

7. Pour the egg mixture into the pan and stir it constantly with the wooden spoon to keep the eggs from burning. The egg mixture will be runny at first but will slowly begin to turn firm as it cooks.

8. Keep stirring. Once the eggs are all firm, the dish is ready.

9. Be sure to turn off the stove.

**FINAL PREPARATION STEP FOR ADULTS:**
Check to be sure the eggs are fully cooked before serving.

**Donna Pettigrew, Anderson, Indiana**
Tanglewood Camp Director and Master Trainer
Girl Scouts of Central Indiana

**DANGER ZONE:**
- Sharp utensils! Careful chopping required.
- Raw eggs! Sanitize your hands after handling.
- Hot and heavy cookware! Keep frying pan handle turned inward.

## Smokey Bear's Berry Pancakes

**INGREDIENTS**

1 cup frozen blueberries

2 cups Aunt Jemima Original Complete pancake and waffle mix

1½ cups water

¼ cup (½ standard stick) butter

¼ cup confectioners' sugar

Maple syrup to taste

"During the 1940s the National Forest Service launched a forest fire prevention campaign that featured posters of a cute bear cub named Smokey. Later, in 1950, a real cub was rescued from a tree during a forest fire in New Mexico. The rescued cub was originally named Hotfoot Teddy because his paws had been burned in the fire. But later his name was changed to Smokey in honor of the bear in the forest fire prevention posters. Smokey the Bear quickly became a real-life celebrity and spent the rest of his life entertaining visitors at the National Zoo in Washington, D.C."

**REQUIRED EQUIPMENT:**

Cookstove
Large mixing bowl
Wooden spoon
Medium-size frying pan
Spatula

**INITIAL PREPARATION STEPS FOR ADULTS:**

1. About 30 to 60 minutes before starting breakfast, set the blueberries out to thaw if they are still frozen.

2. Prepare cookstove for the Scouts.

**PREPARATION STEPS FOR YOUNG SCOUTS:**

1. Pour the pancake mix into a large bowl, then add the water to the bowl. Mix well with a wooden spoon until no large lumps remain in the batter.

2. Add the blueberries to the batter and stir well once again.

Servings: 6 to 8
Preparation Time—Total: 45 minutes
Preparation Time—For the Scouts: 45 minutes
Recommended Number of Chefs: 1 Scout and 1 adult
Challenge Level: Moderate

3. Melt a 1 inch thick chunk of the butter in a medium-size frying pan over low to medium heat on the stove. Move the butter around with the wooden spoon while it melts to cover all the inside of the pan. If the butter starts to sizzle, the pan is too hot so reduce the heat.

4. Pour some batter into the hot frying pan. Using a measuring cup can make this step easier. Be sure to scoop up some of the blueberries too, because they tend to sink to the bottom of the batter in the bowl. Pour just enough batter to make a cake about 6 inches in diameter. The batter will spread out after you pour it, so don't put too much into the pan. Until you get used to making pancakes, cook only one at a time.

5. Once many bubbles form in the top of the pancake, use a spatula to quickly flip the pancake over. Practice makes perfect with this step!

6. Cook for only a short period of time on the second side. Usually about a minute is all that's needed.

7. Move the pancake to a serving tray, then repeat the last three steps—pouring some batter into the pan and cooking the pancake on both sides—until all the batter is used up. Melt more butter in the pan as it's used up.

8. Sprinkle confectioners' sugar over the pancakes when serving. Cover with maple syrup.

**Tim and Christine Conners, Statesboro, Georgia**
Committee Members and Merit Badge Counselors
Troop 340, Coastal Empire Council

**DANGER ZONE:**
- Hot and heavy cookware! Keep frying pan handle turned inward.

**HOT TIP!**
Cooking perfect pancakes is not so easy. Just be sure to look for the bubbles before flipping the cake. Don't forget that it takes much less time to cook the second side.

# Forest Ranger French Toast

## INGREDIENTS

1 dozen eggs

2 cups half-and-half

1 teaspoon vanilla extract

1 loaf French bread

½ cup (1 standard stick) butter

Confectioners' sugar to taste

Maple syrup to taste

"When visiting a state or national park, there's a good chance of crossing paths with a ranger. Of course, rangers aren't only found in forests, but also at beaches, islands, lakes, and deserts. They perform a remarkable variety of jobs. Sometimes they enforce park rules like a police officer. Other times they make sure visitors are driving safely, have their permits, and are following fire regulations. Sometimes they teach visitors about the plants and animals found in their park. If you become lost in a park, rangers will help find you. So here's to the men and women in uniform who do so much to make our parks fun and safe places to visit!"

### REQUIRED EQUIPMENT:
Cookstove
Large mixing bowl
Wooden spoon
Bread knife
Medium-size frying pan
Spatula

### INITIAL PREPARATION STEP FOR ADULTS:
Prepare cookstove for the Scouts.

### PREPARATION STEPS FOR YOUNG SCOUTS:

1. Crack the eggs into a large bowl, then mix them by stirring very quickly with a fork.

2. Pour the half-and-half into the bowl with the eggs.

3. Add the vanilla extract to the eggs and milk in the bowl, then stir well with a wooden spoon.

4. Cut a loaf of French bread into slices about ½ to 1 inch thick using a bread knife. Do this gently. Try not to mash the bread loaf while slicing it.

Servings: 8 to 10
Preparation Time—Total: 45 minutes
Preparation Time—For the Scouts: 45 minutes
Recommended Number of Chefs: 2 Scouts and 1 adult
Challenge Level: Moderate

5. Cut off a chunk of butter about an inch long and melt it over low heat in a medium-size frying pan on the stove. Move the melting butter around with the wooden spoon to cover all the inside of the pan.

6. Move the large bowl close to the frying pan.

7. With clean hands, dip a slice of bread into the egg mixture in the bowl and submerge it so that both sides are coated.

8. Place the slice of coated bread in the hot frying pan. Dip one or two more slices of bread in the same way and add them to the pan. Fill the pan with slices, but don't overcrowd it.

9. Cook the bread until golden brown, but don't allow it to burn. Flip each slice with a spatula, then cook the opposite side in the same way.

10. Move the cooked French toast to a serving tray, then melt a little more butter in the pan.

11. Continue dipping slices in the egg mixture and then cooking them on both sides until all the bread has been cooked.

12. Lightly sprinkle confectioners' sugar over the French toast and serve it with maple syrup.

**Tim and Christine Conners, Statesboro, Georgia**
Committee Members and Merit Badge Counselors
Troop 340, Coastal Empire Council

**Chef's Corner**
This classic French toast recipe really shows just how versatile the egg is for making so many kinds of great foods that we often take for granted.

**DANGER ZONE:**

- Raw eggs! Sanitize your hands after handling.
- Sharp utensils! Careful slicing required.
- Hot and heavy cookware! Keep frying pan handle turned inward.

# Campfire Sausage Sandwich

**INGREDIENTS PER SERVING**
1 English muffin

1 fully cooked sausage patty

1 slice cheddar cheese

**REQUIRED EQUIPMENT:**
Folding camp grill (if fire pit doesn't have a grate)
Bread knife
Heavy-duty aluminum foil
Long-handled tongs

**INITIAL PREPARATION STEPS FOR ADULTS:**

1. Prepare a wood fire well in advance of mealtime, giving the fire time to die down to a low bed of embers.

2. Move the fire pit's grill grate into position over the fire. If the fire pit doesn't have a built-in grate, set up a folding camp grill over the embers.

3. Be prepared to show the Scouts how to properly split an English muffin in the first step below.

**PREPARATION STEPS FOR YOUNG SCOUTS:**

1. Split each English muffin into two rounds, as you would a bagel. If they aren't pre-cut and can't be split by hand, then use a bread knife.

2. Place a sausage patty on the cut side of one of the muffin slices, then set a slice of cheese on top of the sausage.

3. Set the other muffin slice on top, the cut side facing the cheese, to form a sandwich.

4. Tear off a sheet of foil and completely wrap the sausage sandwich in it.

5. Place the wrapped sandwich on a grill grate over the embers in the fire.

6. Cook the sandwich for about 3 to 5 minutes, then flip it with tongs and cook for another 3 to 5 minutes. The sandwich is ready to serve once the cheese is melted.

**DANGER ZONE:**

- Live fire! Use barbecue gloves while working with a wood fire.

- Sharp utensils! Careful slicing required.

**Tim and Christine Conners, Statesboro, Georgia**
Committee Members and Merit Badge Counselors
Troop 340, Coastal Empire Council

Servings: 1—multiply as required
Preparation Time—Total: 1 hour and 15 minutes (including 1 hour to prepare the fire)
Preparation Time—For the Scouts: 15 minutes
Recommended Number of Chefs: 1 Scout and 1 adult
Challenge Level: Easy

# Hot Air Whiz-and-Spam

"I was once on a recovery team that caught descending hot air balloons during their graceful landings. These flights usually occurred at the break of dawn, when the air was most calm, so we didn't have time to eat a proper breakfast prior to the event. It became a tradition on our team that the balloonist would provide the recovery crew with breakfast after their work was done. The pilot would normally bring canned or packaged foods. It was on one such occasion that the team was served Whiz and Spam. We all thought it was the best meal ever!"

## INGREDIENTS
1 (12-ounce) can Spam

1 (8-ounce) jar Cheez Whiz

**REQUIRED EQUIPMENT:**
Chef's knife
2 small bowls
Box of toothpicks

**DANGER ZONE:**
• Sharp utensils! Careful slicing required.

**PREPARATION STEPS FOR YOUNG SCOUTS:**

1. Pop the lid on the Spam and remove the slab of meat from the can.

2. Turn the Spam on its side, then use a chef's knife to slice the meat into bite-size cubes.

3. Place the cubes of Spam in one bowl, then pour the Cheez Whiz into a second bowl.

4. Pass the toothpicks around to the Scouts and leaders.

5. Have the diners spear the cubes of Spam with the toothpicks and then dip them into the Cheez Whiz!

**Rae Bissell, Haverford Township, Pennsylvania**
Former Patrol Leader
Troop 132, Valley Forge Council

HOT TIP!
Spam is a precooked meat product, which is why you can serve it without heating it. Don't try this recipe with raw meat! If you did, you could become very ill.

Servings: 4 to 6
Preparation Time—Total: 15 minutes
Preparation Time—For the Scouts: 15 minutes
Recommended Number of Chefs: 1 Scout and 1 adult
Challenge Level: Easy

# Hawaiian Surfer Pizza

## INGREDIENTS

1 (20-ounce) can sliced pineapple

5 English muffins

1 individual (5-ounce) packet Boboli pizza sauce

10 slices smoked (fully cooked) Canadian bacon or ham

10 slices mozzarella cheese

**HOT TIP!**
Be certain to use fully cooked bacon or ham for this recipe because the cooking time in not adequate when using raw meat!

## REQUIRED EQUIPMENT:

12-inch camp Dutch oven
Briquettes and accessories for Dutch oven
Can opener
Bread knife
Spatula

## INITIAL PREPARATION STEPS FOR ADULTS:

1. Prepare 25 briquettes for the Dutch oven, then preheat oven for about 10 minutes using 17 coals on a metal tray underneath and 8 coals on the lid.

2. Be prepared to show the Scouts how to properly split an English muffin in the second step below.

## PREPARATION STEPS FOR YOUNG SCOUTS:

1. Thoroughly drain the juice from a can of pineapple slices. Do this while an adult prepares the Dutch oven.

2. Split each English muffin into two rounds, as you would a bagel. If they aren't pre-cut and can't be split by hand then use a bread knife.

3. Lay the English muffin halves on a clean surface with the smooth sides of the muffins facing downward and the cut sides facing up.

4. Cut open a corner of the packet of pizza sauce and squirt about a tablespoon of sauce onto each of the muffin halves. The amount doesn't have to be exact, but you'll need to prepare ten muffin halves with the packet of sauce, so keep track of how much sauce you're using on each muffin and adjust if you have to, so you don't run out.

5. Cover each muffin half with a slice of smoked Canadian bacon or ham, then top the bacon or ham with a pineapple ring.

6. Top the pineapple ring on each pizza half with a slice of mozzarella cheese.

Servings: 5
Preparation Time—Total: 45 minutes
Preparation Time—For the Scouts: 30 minutes
Recommended Number of Chefs: 2 Scouts and 1 adult
Challenge Level: Easy

## FINAL PREPARATION STEPS FOR ADULTS:

1. Set the assembled pizzas in the hot Dutch oven using a spatula. Note that 6 pizza halves (3 servings) will fit in a standard 12-inch Dutch oven.

2. Replace lid and bake for about 15 minutes or until cheese fully melts.

3. Continue to cook in batches until all pizzas have been baked.

**Donna Pettigrew, Anderson, Indiana**
Tanglewood Camp Director and Master Trainer
Girl Scouts of Central Indiana

Like Hawaiian pizza, only easier. *Christine Conners*

## INGREDIENTS

**8 hot dogs**

**6 green onions**

**4 (3-ounce) packets ramen noodles, your choice of flavor**

**6 cups water**

# "Squid" and Noodles

"This recipe is sure to get a few laughs. Once the hot dogs are cut into strips, they curl in the pot to look just like squids!"

### REQUIRED EQUIPMENT:

Cookstove
Paring knife
Chef's knife
Medium-size cook pot
Wooden spoon
Long-handled tongs

### INITIAL PREPARATION STEPS FOR ADULTS:

1. Prepare cookstove.

2. The slicing method required in the first few steps is likely to be confusing to the Scouts at first. Be prepared to demonstrate the technique.

### PREPARATION STEPS FOR YOUNG SCOUTS:

1. Use a paring knife to slice a hot dog lengthwise from one end to about halfway down along its length. Don't cut it along the entire length, or it will fall apart.

2. The cut end of the hot dog now consists of two flaps. Using the paring knife, slit each flap down its length two or three more times to turn it into strips that are still joined to the uncut end of the hot dog. This bundle of strips will be the "tentacles" or arms of the squid, while the uncut end of the hot dog will be the squid's head.

3. Do this for each of the hot dogs, then place them in a medium-size cook pot.

4. Cut the ragged top parts from the green onions with a chef's knife and throw the ragged pieces away. Remove the stringy roots too. Chop the rest of the onions into small pieces and place them in the pot.

Servings: 8
Preparation Time—Total: 30 minutes
Preparation Time—For the Scouts: 30 minutes
Recommended Number of Chefs: 2 Scouts and 1 adult
Challenge Level: Moderate

5. Add the noodles and flavoring mix from the packets of ramen noodles to the pot, then pour in the 6 cups of water.

6. Place the pot on the stove and set the flame to its highest setting. Bring the water to a boil while stirring occasionally with a wooden spoon.

7. Cook for 3 to 5 minutes until the noodles become soft and the "tentacles" of the hot dog squids begin to curl.

8. Turn off the stove.

**FINAL PREPARATION STEP FOR ADULTS:**
Use tongs to remove the hot dogs from the pot, then assist with serving the hot noodles.

**Ken Harbison, Rochester, New York**
Former Boy Scout
Washington Trails Council

**DANGER ZONE:**

• Sharp utensils! Careful slicing and chopping required.

• Hot pot! Turn the handle inward and be careful not to spill contents.

Slice the hot dogs in the right way, and they curl up like squids! *Christine Conners*

# Scrambled Chili Dogs

"This recipe originated in an Auburn, Alabama, restaurant circa 1975."

## INGREDIENTS

2 small white onions

8 beef hot dogs

3 (15-ounce) cans no-bean chili

8 hot dog buns

1 (8-ounce) package shredded cheddar cheese

## REQUIRED EQUIPMENT:

Cookstove
Chef's knife
Small bowl
Medium-size cook pot
Can opener
Wooden spoon

## INITIAL PREPARATION STEP FOR ADULTS:

Prepare cookstove.

## PREPARATION STEPS FOR YOUNG SCOUTS:

1. Use a chef's knife to cut the stem and root part from the top and bottom of the onions, then peel off the dry skin.

2. Set the onions on a flat end where the stem or root part was removed to keep them from rolling, then chop them into small pieces. Place the chopped onions in a small bowl.

3. Slice the hot dogs into disks, each about as thick as your pinky finger. Place the sliced hot dogs in a medium-size cook pot.

4. Pour the cans of chili into the pot.

5. Set the stove to a medium flame, about halfway between the lowest and highest settings. Stir occasionally with a wooden spoon until the chili dog mixture is warm. This will take about 5 minutes.

6. Turn the stove off.

7. Arrange eight plates and set a hot dog bun on each. Using clean hands, open each bun and mash it flat!

8. Use the spoon or a ladle to cover each of the buns with some of the chili dog mixture. Top the chili with some of the chopped onions, if desired, then add a handful of shredded cheese.

9. You won't be able to easily eat this chili dog with your fingers, so plan to pass out forks.

## DANGER ZONE:

• Sharp utensils! Careful slicing and chopping required.

• Hot pot! Turn the handle inward and be careful not to spill contents.

Servings: 8
Preparation Time—Total: 30 minutes
Preparation Time—For the Scouts: 30 minutes
Recommended Number of Chefs: 2 Scouts and 1 adult
Challenge Level: Moderate

**Steve Burleson, Irondale, Alabama**
Assistant Scoutmaster
Troop 213, Greater Alabama Council

# Bigfoot Macaroni

**REQUIRED EQUIPMENT:**
Cookstove
Large cook pot
Chef's knife
Medium-size mixing bowl
Wooden spoon
Can opener

**INITIAL PREPARATION STEPS FOR ADULTS:**

1. Prepare cookstove.

2. Fill a large pot halfway full with water and bring to a boil.

3. Be ready to help the Scouts drain hot water from the pasta once it's finished cooking.

**PREPARATION STEPS FOR YOUNG SCOUTS:**

1. Cut the lumps of broccoli from the end of each stem. Chop the lumps and thin stems into small pieces and place in a bowl. Throw away the larger pieces of stem. Do this while the adult prepares the boiling water.

2. Chop the ham into cubes a little smaller than the size of dice. Add the ham to the bowl with the broccoli.

3. Pour the elbow macaroni into the boiling water and stir for a few seconds with a wooden spoon.

4. Continue to boil the macaroni until it becomes soft. This will take about 10 minutes. Occasionally taste the macaroni to see if it's done.

5. Once the macaroni is soft, turn off the stove, then ask an adult to help with draining the hot water from the pot. Do not drain the water yourself!

6. Once the water is drained, place the pot with the macaroni in it back on the stove. If the pot is still too heavy, ask an adult for help!

**INGREDIENTS**

1 head broccoli

1 pound smoked ham

1 (16-ounce) package elbow macaroni

1 (8-ounce) can sliced mushrooms

1 cup whole milk

10 slices American cheese

Servings: 8 to 10
Preparation Time—Total: 30 minutes
Preparation Time—For the Scouts: 30 minutes
Recommended Number of Chefs: 2 Scouts and 1 adult
Challenge Level: Moderate

7. Drain the water from the can of mushrooms and add them to the pasta in the pot.

8. Add the milk and the slices of American cheese to the pot. Use the wooden spoon to stir until the milk is mixed.

9. Pour the broccoli and ham into the pot. Stir well again.

10. Turn the stove back on and set it to a low flame. Warm pasta until the cheese melts and the broccoli is heated through, about five to ten minutes. Occasionally stir the pasta to keep it from burning.

11. Turn off the stove.

## FINAL PREPARATION STEP FOR ADULTS:
Help the Scouts move the hot pot to the serving area once it's ready.

**Scott Simerly, Apex, North Carolina**
Senior Assistant Scoutmaster
Troop 204, Occoneechee Council

---

**Chef's Corner**

The green lumps at the end of broccoli stems are actually flower buds that have yet to bloom. They are called florets.

---

**DANGER ZONE:**

• Boiling water! An adult must drain large pots.

• Sharp utensils! Careful chopping required.

• Hot and heavy cookware! Be careful not to spill contents.

# Nachos to Go

## REQUIRED EQUIPMENT:
Cookstove
Chef's knife
3 medium-size bowls
Can opener
Small cook pot
Wooden spoon
Small bowl
Ladle

## INITIAL PREPARATION STEPS FOR ADULTS:
1. Prepare cookstove.

2. Be sure the chili isn't too hot when the Scouts are ladling it into the Dorito bags.

## PREPARATION STEPS FOR YOUNG SCOUTS:
1. Cut the tops and bottoms off the tomatoes with a chef's knife. Throw away the tops and bottoms, then slice and chop what remains of the tomato into small cubes. Place the chopped tomato in a medium-size bowl.

2. If an adult hasn't done so already, cut off about ¼ of a head of lettuce. Don't cut through the stem when doing this. Take the large piece of lettuce you've removed, and slice and chop it into shreds. Place the lettuce shreds in a second bowl.

3. Dump the shredded cheese into a third bowl.

4. Open the can of chili and pour the contents into a small cook pot, then warm it over a low flame on the stove. Stir the chili occasionally while it cooks, using a wooden spoon. Don't allow the chili to become boiling hot! Once the chili is warm, turn off the stove.

## INGREDIENTS
2 tomatoes

¼ head iceberg lettuce

1 (8-ounce) package shredded cheese, your choice

1 (15-ounce) can chili

6 single-serving packages Doritos

1 (8-ounce) container sour cream

Servings: 6
Preparation Time—Total: 45 minutes
Preparation Time—For the Scouts: 45 minutes
Recommended Number of Chefs: 2 Scouts and 1 adult
Challenge Level: Moderate

5. Smash each bag of Doritos while they are still sealed so that the chips become small pieces you can feel through the bag. Don't mash so hard that the bags blow open.

6. Open a bag of Doritos and set the bag inside a small bowl so that it won't tip over. Using a ladle, scoop about ¼ cup of warm chili into the bag. Be careful not to spill.

7. Using a measuring cup, add about ⅓ cup of shredded cheese to the bag.

8. Repeat the last two steps, opening each of the remaining bags and adding chili and cheese. As you finish each bag, hand it to a Scout.

9. Tell the Scouts to add their own chopped tomatoes, chopped lettuce, and sour cream to their bags. They can eat directly from the bag using a fork.

**James Landis, New Providence, Pennsylvania**
Unit Commissioner
Conestoga River District, Pennsylvania Dutch Council

HOT TIP!
This recipe has a lot of steps that make it more challenging than you might think for first-time chefs. But once they get the hang of it, it's easy.

# Sloppy Joes

**REQUIRED EQUIPMENT:**
Cookstove
Medium-size frying pan
Wooden spoon

**INITIAL PREPARATION STEP FOR ADULTS:**
Prepare cookstove for the Scouts.

**PREPARATION STEPS FOR YOUNG SCOUTS:**
1. Place a medium-size frying pan on the stove, then set the flame to medium, halfway between the lowest and highest settings.

2. Add the ground beef to the skillet and begin breaking apart the lumps with a wooden spoon. Keep stirring as the pan becomes hot, to keep the beef from burning.

3. Continue to break apart the lumps of beef while stirring. Once the meat has become gray in color with no hint of pink remaining, add the yellow mustard and the ketchup to the pan. Stir everything well with the spoon.

4. Add the brown sugar to the beef and stir until well mixed. Cook for another minute, then turn off the stove.

5. Serve the sloppy joe mixture on buns. This can be a pretty messy business. It's easier to place a single bun on a plate first, then scoop some of the beef mixture onto the bun using the wooden spoon. Repeat for each of the diners.

**FINAL PREPARATION STEP FOR ADULTS:**
Be certain that the ground beef has been thoroughly cooked before serving.

**Donna Pettigrew, Anderson, Indiana**
Tanglewood Camp Director and Master Trainer
Girl Scouts of Central Indiana

**INGREDIENTS**
1 pound lean ground beef

1 tablespoon prepared (yellow) mustard

½ cup ketchup

¼ cup brown sugar

6 hamburger buns

**DANGER ZONE:**
- Raw meat! Sanitize your hands after handling.
- Hot and heavy cookware! Keep frying pan handle turned inward.

Servings: 6
Preparation Time—Total: 30 minutes
Preparation Time—For the Scouts: 30 minutes
Recommended Number of Chefs: 1 Scout and 1 adult
Challenge Level: Moderate

# Cheese Dog on a Fork

"This is a fun open-fire lunch that doesn't require much clean-up."

### INGREDIENTS

1 (16.3-ounce) container Pillsbury Original Home-style Grands! refrigerated biscuits

8 cheese-filled regular-length hot dogs

Optional: squeeze ketchup and mustard

### DANGER ZONE:

- Live fire! Use barbecue gloves while working with a wood fire.
- Sharp points! Keep the camping forks away from faces.
- Hot steam! Allow the food to cool for a few minutes before eating.

### REQUIRED EQUIPMENT:

Camping forks, one for each of the Scouts

### INITIAL PREPARATION STEP FOR ADULTS:

Prepare a wood fire well in advance of mealtime, perhaps even using the embers left over from the morning fire.

### PREPARATION STEPS FOR YOUNG SCOUTS:

1. Open the container of biscuit dough and separate the biscuits from each other. There will be eight of them.

2. Shape each biscuit dough into a log about 6 inches long.

3. Set a hot dog into the dough log, then wrap the dough completely around the hot dog. Pinch the sides and ends of the dough together to seal it shut. Do this for each dog.

4. Spear each dough-covered hot dog with a camping fork.

5. Hold the dough-covered dog over the hot embers and rotate the fork often to cook all sides of the dough.

6. Heat the dough until it becomes golden brown all over. Move the hot dog away from the fire, then patiently hold the camping fork for a few minutes while the bread and hot dog cool a little.

7. If desired, add ketchup or mustard before eating.

### FINAL PREPARATION STEP FOR ADULTS:

It's easy to burn your mouth by biting into hot roasted food if it hasn't had time to lose some heat. Make sure that the Scouts each give their dog a few minutes to cool off.

**James Landis, New Providence, Pennsylvania**
Unit Commissioner
Conestoga River District, Pennsylvania
Dutch Council

Servings: 8

Preparation Time—Total: 1 hour and 30 minutes (including 1 hour to prepare the fire)

Preparation Time—For the Scouts: 30 minutes

Recommended Number of Chefs: 1 Scout per serving and 1 adult

Challenge Level: Moderate

# Kampin' Kebabs

**REQUIRED EQUIPMENT:**
Folding camp grill (if fire pit doesn't have a grate)
Chef's knife
Medium-size mixing bowl
3 small bowls
Can opener
12 (1-foot-long) wooden skewers
Basting brush
Long-handled tongs

## INGREDIENTS
16 ounces frozen pre-cooked chicken nuggets

1 green bell pepper

1 red bell pepper

1 sweet onion

1 (20-ounce) can pine-apple chunks

1 (12.8-ounce) jar teriyaki baste and glaze

## INITIAL PREPARATION STEPS FOR ADULTS:
1. Prepare a wood fire well in advance of mealtime, perhaps even using the embers left over from the morning fire.

2. Move the fire pit's grill grate into position over the fire. If the fire pit doesn't have a built-in grate, set up a folding camp grill over the embers.

3. About an hour before lunchtime, set the chicken nuggets out to thaw if they are still frozen.

4. About 30 minutes before lunchtime, place the wooden skewers in water to soak. This will help prevent them from burning over the fire.

5. Be prepared to keep an eye on the Scouts as they thread the skewers, to be sure that they balance the chicken with the vegetables and pineapple.

## PREPARATION STEPS FOR YOUNG SCOUTS:
1. Remove the top stem-part from both a green and a red bell pepper. Next, cut the peppers in half, remove the seeds, then scrape out the white "ribs" on the inside. Slice what's left of the peppers into bite-size squares and place them in a medium-size bowl.

Servings: 6
Preparation Time—Total: 1 hour and 45 minutes
(including 1 hour to prepare the fire)
Preparation Time—For the Scouts: 45 minutes
Recommended Number of Chefs: 3 Scouts and 1 adult
Challenge Level: Difficult

**DANGER ZONE:**

- Live fire! Use barbecue gloves while working with a wood fire.

- Sharp points! Keep the camping forks away from faces.

- Sharp utensils! Careful chopping required.

2. Cut the stem and root part from the top and bottom of the onion, then peel off the dry skin. Also peel off the first layer of the onion under the dry skin.

3. Set the onion on a flat end where the stem or root part was removed. This will help keep it from rolling while you slice. Cut the onion into thick slices, then cut the slices into bite-size squares. Place the onion pieces in a small bowl.

4. Drain the liquid from the can of pineapple. Pour the pineapple chunks into another small bowl.

5. Thread the chicken nuggets, bell peppers, onions, and pineapple onto the skewers. Mix up the ingredients on each skewer. In other words, don't load some with only chicken nuggets. Skewer the chicken through the long length of the nugget, not the short length. Otherwise, the nuggets may not hold well on the skewers.

6. Pour some of the teriyaki sauce into a small bowl. Use the basting brush to coat all the items on the skewers with sauce. Pour more teriyaki sauce into the bowl if needed.

7. Place the kebabs on the grill grate over the embers. Use tongs to turn the kebabs every few minutes to keep them from burning.

8. Serve once the nuggets and vegetables are browned. This typically takes about 15 minutes.

**Ken Harbison, Rochester, New York**
Former Boy Scout
Washington Trails Council

# Hiking Roll-Ups

"A fun alternative to the traditional sandwich. Roll-ups are easy to prepare, and they pack well for short day hikes."

**REQUIRED EQUIPMENT:**
None

**PREPARATION STEPS FOR YOUNG SCOUTS:**

1. Lay a tortilla on a clean, flat surface.

2. Arrange 2 slices of cheese on the tortilla, then add 2 slices of deli meat. Keep the meat and cheese away from the edges, so they won't hang out once it's rolled up.

3. Squeeze a little mayonnaise or mustard over the meat and cheese if you like.

4. Roll the tortilla into a tube.

5. Repeat all the above steps for each serving.

**Kathleen Kirby, Milltown, New Jersey**
Merit Badge Counselor
Troop 33, Central New Jersey Council

**INGREDIENTS PER SERVING:**

1 (6-inch) flour tortilla

2 slices cheese, your choice

2 slices deli meat, your choice

Optional: squeeze mayonnaise and mustard

*HOT TIP!*
If the roll-ups are to be taken along for lunch on a day hike, wrap each tightly in foil. To avoid spoilage, don't delay in eating them, especially if the day is warm.

Servings: 1—multiply as required
Preparation Time—Total: 5 minutes
Preparation Time—For the Scouts: 5 minutes
Recommended Number of Chefs: 1 Scout per serving and 1 adult
Challenge Level: Easy

# Chicken Caesar Salad

## INGREDIENTS

1 (22-ounce) package Tyson Grilled & Ready chicken breast chunks

1 (10-ounce) package precut romaine lettuce

1 (5- to 6-ounce) package croutons

6 ounces (about 1½ cups) grated Parmesan cheese

8 ounces Caesar salad dressing

### REQUIRED EQUIPMENT:
Large bowl
Long-handled tongs

### INITIAL PREPARATION STEP FOR ADULTS:
If the chicken is frozen, set the package in a warm location to thaw about 1 to 2 hours before lunch.

### PREPARATION STEPS FOR YOUNG SCOUTS:
1. Dump the romaine lettuce into a large bowl.

2. Pour the entire bag of chicken into the bowl along with the package of croutons and the grated Parmesan cheese.

3. Use tongs to "toss" the salad to mix up the ingredients.

4. Pour the Caesar dressing over the salad in the bowl and use the tongs once more to toss and mix the ingredients together before serving.

**Ken Harbison, Rochester, New York**
Former Boy Scout
Washington Trails Council

---

**Chef's Corner**
To "toss" a salad means to use tongs or large salad forks to gently grab, lift, and mix a salad so that all the ingredients are jumbled together before serving.

---

Servings: 6 to 8
Preparation Time—Total: 15 minutes
Preparation Time—For the Scouts: 15 minutes
Recommended Number of Chefs: 1 Scout and 1 adult
Challenge Level: Easy

# Viking Tuna Sandwiches

"The Vikings are remembered as a fierce seafaring people from Scandinavia that tromped the Earth between the eighth and eleventh centuries A.D. While probably most famous for raiding and pillaging, they were also skilled traders, explorers, and colonists who left an enduring mark on European history."

## REQUIRED EQUIPMENT:

Chef's knife
Paring knife
Medium-size mixing bowl
Wooden spoon

## INITIAL PREPARATION STEP FOR ADULTS:

Slicing apples can be a challenge, especially when the cores are tough. Assist the Scouts as needed with this preparation step and be sure the seeds are removed.

## PREPARATION STEPS FOR YOUNG SCOUTS:

1. Use a chef's knife to cut an apple in half from top to bottom, then slice each of these pieces in half from top to bottom. You'll have four pieces at this point.

2. Remove the core and seeds from each piece of apple using a paring knife.

3. Use the chef's knife to chop the apple wedges into small pieces about the size of your pinky fingernail.

4. Mix the mayonnaise and the curry powder in a medium-size bowl with a wooden spoon.

5. Add the apple pieces to the bowl along with the dried cranberries and cashew pieces. Mix everything well.

6. Open the four sandwich thins. Spoon the tuna mixture onto one half of each sandwich thin. Try to divide the mixture evenly between the four. Top each filled half of a sandwich thin with its other half, then serve.

**Ken Harbison, Rochester, New York**
Former Boy Scout
Washington Trails Council

## INGREDIENTS

2 (6- to 7-ounce) packages tuna

1 medium-size apple

⅓ cup light mayonnaise

1 teaspoon curry powder

⅓ cup dried cranberries

⅓ cup cashew pieces

4 sandwich thins

### DANGER ZONE:

• Sharp utensils! Careful chopping required.

Servings: 4
Preparation Time—Total: 30 minutes
Preparation Time—For the Scouts: 30 minutes
Recommended Number of Chefs: 1 Scout and 1 adult
Challenge Level: Moderate

# Walking Salad

## INGREDIENTS

6 medium-size apples

½ cup peanut butter

¼ cup honey

¼ cup raisins or roasted peanuts

## REQUIRED EQUIPMENT:

Paring knife

Narrow metal spoon

Quart-size ziplock freezer bag

## INITIAL PREPARATION STEP FOR ADULTS:

Assist the Scouts with coring the apples. This step is tricky because the bottom of each apple needs to remain intact. Make an initial circular cut with a paring knife at the top of the apple, then dig the core out using a narrow spoon. Remember not to puncture the bottom of the apple.

## PREPARATION STEPS FOR YOUNG SCOUTS:

1. Scoop the peanut butter into a quart-size ziplock bag. Have another person hold the bag open while you do this to keep the peanut butter from getting all over the seal.

2. Next, pour the honey into the bag with the peanut butter. The amount doesn't have to be accurate.

3. Add the raisins or roasted peanuts to the bag.

4. Seal the bag tightly while squeezing the air out, then carefully mash the ingredients together in the bag until they are well mixed.

5. Pinch a bottom corner of the ziplock bag to move the peanut butter mix out of it, then cut the corner off using a pair of scissors or a small knife. The corner cut should be about ½ inch long.

6. Squeeze the peanut butter mix through the cut corner of the bottom of the bag into the hollowed-out space in each of the apples.

7. Serve the apples immediately or wrap in foil for the trail.

**Donna Pettigrew, Anderson, Indiana**
Tanglewood Camp Director and Master Trainer
Girl Scouts of Central Indiana

### DANGER ZONE:

- Sharp utensils! Careful slicing required.

### Chef's Corner

The walking salad is a favorite Scout recipe with many variations that have been around for years.

Servings: 6

Preparation Time—Total: 30 minutes

Preparation Time—For the Scouts: 30 minutes

Recommended Number of Chefs: 2 Scouts and 1 adult

Challenge Level: Moderate

# Fruit Trees with Dip

## REQUIRED EQUIPMENT:
Chef's knife
At least 4 small bowls
Medium-size mixing bowl
Wooden spoon
8 (1-foot-long) skewers

## INITIAL PREPARATION STEP FOR ADULTS:
The skewers are to be loaded with small pieces of fruit, just as one would prepare shish kebab. Depending on the fruit available, some, like melons and pineapples, will require peeling, coring, and cubing. Others, like grapes, will require no preparation at all. Determine the level of cutting required for the fruit available, then assign light-duty jobs to the Scouts, such as cubing pre-cored apples or peeling kiwis, and handle heavy-duty jobs, such as removing the rind from melons, yourself.

## PREPARATION STEPS FOR YOUNG SCOUTS:
1. Peel and cut up the fruit as directed by the adult. Place each type of fruit in its own small bowl. For example, put all the apple cubes in one and all the banana chunks in another, and so on.
2. Take a medium-size bowl, one with no fruit in it, and pour the yogurt into it. Next, add the whipped topping to the yogurt. Stir the yogurt and whipped topping together using a wooden spoon.
3. Instruct all of the diners to thoroughly wash their hands.
4. Hand a skewer to each of the diners and have them load their "fruit trees" with a variety of their favorite fruits from the small bowls.
5. Have the diners dip their fruit into the yogurt-topping mixture before eating, if they'd like.

## INGREDIENTS
**A selection of at least four 1-pound servings of these fruit options:**

**Bananas**

**Pineapple**

**Melon**

**Grapes**

**Strawberries**

**Maraschino cherries**

**Large blueberries**

**Large blackberries**

**Kiwis**

**Apples**

**Plums**

**Apricots**

**Peaches**

**1 (8-ounce) container yogurt (any flavor)**

**1 (8-ounce) container whipped topping**

Servings: 8
Preparation Time—Total: 30 minutes
Preparation Time—For the Scouts: 30 minutes
Recommended Number of Chefs: 3 Scouts and 1 adult
Challenge Level: Easy

### FINAL PREPARATION STEP FOR ADULTS:

To avoid spreading germs, be certain that all diners wash their hands in advance and that any fruit they touch becomes theirs and isn't placed back in the bowl if they decide on something else. Also be sure that no diners "double-dip" their skewers into the yogurt dip once they begin eating their fruit.

**Tim and Christine Conners, Statesboro, Georgia**
Committee Members and Merit Badge Counselors
Troop 340, Coastal Empire Council

**DANGER ZONE:**

- Sharp utensils! Careful chopping required.
- Germs! All diners must have clean hands.
- Sharp points! Keep the skewers away from faces.

HOT TIP!
Have the Scouts stab their fruit cubes with their skewers. It's fun for them and helps to avoid spreading germs.

# Cheese Puppy Pie

*"Tastes like a real hot dog, only better!"*

## REQUIRED EQUIPMENT:
12-inch camp Dutch oven with trivet
Briquettes and accessories for Dutch oven
Chef's knife
Medium-size bowl
Large mixing bowl
Wooden spoon
Deep 9-inch pie pan

## INITIAL PREPARATION STEP FOR ADULTS:
Prepare 29 briquettes for the Dutch oven.

## PREPARATION STEPS FOR YOUNG SCOUTS:
1. Chop the hot dogs into small pieces and place them in a medium-size bowl. Do this while an adult prepares the coals for the Dutch oven.

2. Cut the stem and root part from the top and bottom of the onion, then peel off the dry skin. Also peel off the first layer of the onion under the dry skin.

3. Set the onion on a flat end where the stem or root part was removed. This will help keep it from rolling while you slice and then chop it into small pieces. Place the chopped onion in the bowl with the hot dogs.

4. Crack the eggs into a large bowl, not the bowl containing the hot dogs and onions.

5. Add the milk and the salt to the bowl with the eggs.

6. Pour the shredded cheese and the Bisquick into the bowl with the milk and eggs. Stir well with a wooden spoon until most of the lumps are gone.

7. Add the chopped hot dogs and onions to the large bowl. Stir well once more.

## INGREDIENTS
1 (16-ounce) package hot dogs

1 medium onion

2 eggs

1 cup milk

½ teaspoon salt

1 cup shredded cheddar cheese

½ cup Heart Smart Bisquick

Optional: ketchup, mustard, or relish

Servings: 5 to 7
Preparation Time—Total: 1 hour
Preparation Time—For the Scouts: 30 minutes
Recommended Number of Chefs: 2 Scouts and 1 adult
Challenge Level: Moderate

8. Pour this hot dog pie batter into a pie pan.

9. Set the pie pan on a trivet in the oven and replace the lid. If you don't know what a trivet is, ask an adult.

10. Place 19 coals on the lid, leaving 10 briquettes under the oven.

## FINAL PREPARATION STEPS FOR ADULTS:

1. Bake for 30 to 40 minutes, until the batter becomes firm.

2. Serve with optional ketchup, mustard, or relish.

**Kathleen Kirby, Milltown, New Jersey**
Merit Badge Counselor
Troop 33, Central New Jersey Council

## DANGER ZONE:

- Hot coals! Enforce your fire-safe zone and use your gloves.

- Sharp utensils! Careful chopping required.

- Raw eggs! Sanitize your hands after handling.

- Hot and heavy cookware! Use your gloves.

**HOT TIP!**
This recipe is also perfect for cooking in a box oven. See appendix C for details on how to make one. Use enough coals to provide a baking temperature of about 400°F.

# Fisherman's Catch

## REQUIRED EQUIPMENT:
12-inch camp Dutch oven
Briquettes and accessories for Dutch oven
Wooden spoon
Chef's knife

## INITIAL PREPARATION STEP FOR ADULTS:
Prepare 25 briquettes for the Dutch oven.

## PREPARATION STEPS FOR YOUNG SCOUTS:
1. Spray the inside of the Dutch oven with cooking spray. Do this while an adult prepares the coals.

2. Dump the stuffing mix into the Dutch oven.

3. Pour the 1½ cups of water over the stuffing mix in the oven and stir well with a wooden spoon.

4. Use a chef's knife to slice the butter into thin pieces. Lay the butter slices over the stuffing mix in the oven.

5. Lay the fish fillets over the butter and stuffing in the oven.

6. Slice the lemons into thin circles using the knife and lay the lemon circles over the fish fillets.

7. Once the adult says the coals are ready, put the lid on the oven, then set the oven on a metal tray. Place 8 coals under the oven and 17 coals on lid.

8. Bake for about 40 minutes.

**Donna Pettigrew, Anderson, Indiana**
Tanglewood Camp Director and Master Trainer
Girl Scouts of Central Indiana

## INGREDIENTS
Cooking spray

1 (6-ounce) package Betty Crocker Homestyle cornbread stuffing mix

1½ cups water

¼ cup (½ standard stick) butter

2 pounds dressed white fish (tilapia, flounder, trout, sole, haddock, cod, or pollock)

2 lemons

### DANGER ZONE:
- Hot coals! Enforce your fire-safe zone and use your gloves.
- Sharp utensils! Careful slicing and chopping required.
- Hot and heavy cookware! Use your gloves.

Much less messy than a fish fry.
*Christine Conners*

Servings: 6 to 8
Preparation Time—Total: 1 hour
Preparation Time—For the Scouts: 1 hour
Recommended Number of Chefs: 2 Scouts and 1 adult
Challenge Level: Easy

# Cowboy Casserole

## INGREDIENTS

**2 (16-ounce) packages frozen California-style mixed vegetables**

**Vegetable oil for greasing Dutch oven**

**2 stalks celery**

**1 large onion**

**1 pound smoked kielbasa sausage**

**2 (15-ounce) cans sliced new potatoes**

**1 teaspoon Lawry's Seasoned Salt**

**1 pound cheddar cheese**

## REQUIRED EQUIPMENT:

12-inch camp Dutch oven
Briquettes and accessories for Dutch oven
Chef's knife
Can opener
Wooden spoon

## INITIAL PREPARATION STEPS FOR ADULTS:

1. About an hour before starting the coals, set the mixed vegetables out to thaw if they are still frozen.

2. Grease Dutch oven with a little vegetable oil.

3. Prepare 25 briquettes.

## PREPARATION STEPS FOR YOUNG SCOUTS:

1. Slice the leafy part from the celery using a chef's knife, then cut off the wide, white bottom part from each stalk. You should have about 6 to 8 inches of usable stalk left for each. Do this while the adult is preparing the coals for the Dutch oven.

2. Cut the celery into thin slices, then chop the slices into small pieces. Put them into the Dutch oven.

3. Cut the stem and root from the top and bottom of the onion, then peel off the dry skin.

4. Set the onion on a flat end where the stem or root part was removed to keep it from rolling, then chop it into small pieces. Place the chopped onion in the oven.

5. Chop the smoked sausage into bite-size pieces and place them in the oven.

6. Pour the packages of mixed vegetables into the oven.

7. Open the cans of sliced potatoes and drain the juice from the cans. You won't need it. Next, pour the potatoes into the oven. Mix everything well with a wooden spoon.

Servings: 8 to 10
Preparation Time—Total: 1 hour
Preparation Time—For the Scouts: 1 hour
Recommended Number of Chefs: 2 Scouts and 1 adult
Challenge Level: Moderate

8. Sprinkle the teaspoon of Lawry's Seasoned Salt over all the food in the oven.

9. Cut the cheddar cheese into slices about ¼ inch thick (the width of your pinky finger). Lay the cheese over the top of the vegetables and sausage in the Dutch oven.

10. Once the adult says the coals are ready, put the lid on the oven, then set the oven on a metal tray. Place 8 coals under the oven and 17 coals on the lid.

11. Cook for about 30 minutes, until the cheese is completely melted.

**Delano LaGow, Oswego, Illinois**
Committee Member
Troop 31, Three Fires Council

### DANGER ZONE:

- Hot coals! Enforce your fire-safe zone and use your gloves.
- Sharp utensils! Careful chopping required.
- Hot and heavy cookware! Use your gloves.

**HOT TIP!**
Rotate a Dutch oven one-quarter of a turn every 15 minutes to keep food from burning over any hot spots. Also rotate the lid one-quarter of a turn for the same reason.

# Dutch Oven Fiesta

## INGREDIENTS

1 medium-size onion

1 pound lean ground beef

1 (1.25-ounce) package taco seasoning mix

1 (14.5-ounce) can diced tomatoes with green chilies

1 (15-ounce) can sweet corn

2 eggs

⅔ cup milk

2 (8.5-ounce) packages Jiffy corn muffin mix

## REQUIRED EQUIPMENT:

12-inch camp Dutch oven
Briquettes and accessories for Dutch oven
Chef's knife
Wooden spoon
Can opener
Medium-size bowl

## INITIAL PREPARATION STEPS FOR ADULTS:

1. Prepare 25 briquettes for the Dutch oven.

2. Warm the oven over all 25 coals on a metal tray.

## PREPARATION STEPS FOR YOUNG SCOUTS:

1. Use a chef's knife to cut the stem and root part from the top and bottom of the onion, then peel off the dry skin. Do this while an adult prepares the Dutch oven.

2. Set the onion on a flat end where the stem or root part was removed to keep it from rolling, then chop it into small pieces.

3. Once the adult says the oven is ready, place the chopped onion in the hot Dutch oven.

4. Add the ground beef to the Dutch oven and begin breaking apart the lumps with a wooden spoon. Stir the beef, mixing it with the onions.

5. Continue to break apart the lumps of beef while stirring often. Once the meat has become gray with no hint of pink remaining, add the package of taco seasoning. Stir well.

6. Add the can of tomatoes with green chilies to the oven.

7. Drain the juice from the can of sweet corn and pour the corn into the oven. Stir everything again.

Servings: 8 to 10
Preparation Time—Total: 1 hour
Preparation Time—For the Scouts: 1 hour
Recommended Number of Chefs: 2 Scouts and 1 adult
Challenge Level: Moderate

8. Crack the eggs into a medium-size bowl. Mix them by stirring very quickly with a fork, then add the milk to the eggs and stir again.

9. Pour both packages of corn muffin mix into the bowl of eggs and milk. Stir well with the wooden spoon until the batter is thick and no large lumps remain.

10. Pour the corn muffin batter over the beef mixture in the oven. Use the spoon to scoop the batter out of the bowl. Don't stir the batter into the beef mixture, just put it on top!

11. Place the lid on the oven, then move 17 coals from under the oven to the lid.

12. Bake for about 30 minutes.

**FINAL PREPARATION STEP FOR ADULTS:**
Help the Scouts determine when the corn muffin topping is ready by showing them how an inserted knife or toothpick should come out clean.

**Charles Flay, Yadkinville, North Carolina**
Unit Commissioner
Pack 699, Old Hickory Council

## DANGER ZONE:

- Hot coals! Enforce your fire-safe zone and use your gloves.

- Sharp utensils! Careful chopping required.

- Raw meat and eggs! Sanitize your hands after handling.

- Hot and heavy cookware! Use your gloves.

## INGREDIENTS
Cooking spray

1 small onion

1 (13-ounce) package tortilla chips

2 (16-ounce) cans refried beans

3 (12.5-ounce) cans chunk chicken

1 (10-ounce) can enchilada sauce

1 (10.75-ounce) can condensed cream of chicken soup

1 (16-ounce) jar mild salsa

1 (8-ounce) package shredded cheddar cheese

# Easy Chicken Enchilada

"Each patrol is supposed to invite a leader to share the evening meal with them. Well, the boys enjoy this recipe very much. On one camping trip, they proceeded to indulge themselves, forgetting the invitation. When they did 'remember,' the chicken enchilada was all but gone. Peanut butter and jelly for me that night!"

### REQUIRED EQUIPMENT:
12-inch camp Dutch oven
Briquettes and accessories for Dutch oven
Chef's knife
Can opener
Medium-size mixing bowl

### INITIAL PREPARATION STEP FOR ADULTS:
Prepare 25 briquettes for the Dutch oven.

### PREPARATION STEPS FOR YOUNG SCOUTS:
1. Spray the inside of the Dutch oven with cooking spray. Do this while an adult prepares the coals.

2. Cut the stem and root part from the top and bottom of a small onion using a chef's knife, then peel off the dry skin. Also peel off the first layer of the onion under the dry skin.

3. Set the onion on a flat end where the stem or root part was removed. This will help keep it from rolling while you slice and then chop it into small pieces.

4. Pour about a third of the bag of tortilla chips into the Dutch oven.

5. Use a spoon to spread both cans of refried beans over the tortilla chips in the oven.

6. Open the cans of chicken and drain the juice. Crumble the chicken over the beans and tortillas in the oven.

7. Sprinkle the chopped onions over the chicken.

Servings: 9 to 11
Preparation Time—Total: 1 hour
Preparation Time—For the Scouts: 1 hour
Recommended Number of Chefs: 2 Scouts and 1 adult
Challenge Level: Easy

8. Dump the can of enchilada sauce and the can of condensed chicken soup into a medium-size bowl and mix with a spoon. Pour the mixture over the ingredients in the oven.

9. Place about half of the remaining tortilla chips over the top of the ingredients in the oven, then pour the jar of salsa over the chips.

10. Top all the ingredients with the shredded cheddar cheese.

11. Once the adult says the coals are ready, put the lid on the oven, then set the oven on a metal tray. Place 8 coals under the oven and 17 coals on lid.

12. Bake for about 40 minutes.

13. Serve with the remaining tortilla chips.

**James Landis, New Providence, Pennsylvania**
Unit Commissioner
Conestoga River District, Pennsylvania Dutch Council

**DANGER ZONE:**

- Hot coals! Enforce your fire-safe zone and use your gloves.

- Sharp utensils! Careful slicing and chopping required.

- Hot and heavy cookware! Use your gloves.

*HOT TIP!*
This is a forgiving recipe. Even if the steps end up jumbled, the results are going to be tasty. And since the meat is precooked, there is no risk from undercooking.

## Davy Crockett's Wild Frontier Chicken Pot Pie

### INGREDIENTS

1 (16-ounce) package frozen mixed vegetables (carrots, peas, corn, and green beans)

3 (10.5-ounce) cans Swanson chicken à la king

1 (22-ounce) package Tyson Grilled & Ready chicken breast chunks

Handful of all-purpose flour

1 (14-ounce, 2-count) package refrigerated pie crust dough

"Davy Crockett was a politician, storyteller, and soldier who died at the infamous Battle of the Alamo in 1836. Stage plays, television shows, movies, and songs have exaggerated his life to mythical proportions. He is an American folk hero best known as the King of the Wild Frontier."

### REQUIRED EQUIPMENT:

12-inch camp Dutch oven
Briquettes and accessories for Dutch oven
Can opener
Wooden spoon
Cutting board
Chef's knife
Large serving spoon

### INITIAL PREPARATION STEPS FOR ADULTS:

1. If they haven't softened already, set the vegetables and chicken breasts in a warm location to thaw about an hour before starting the coals.

2. Prepare 25 briquettes for the Dutch oven.

3. Warm the oven over all 25 coals on a metal tray.

### PREPARATION STEPS FOR YOUNG SCOUTS:

1. Once the adult says the Dutch oven is ready, pour the mixed vegetables, chicken à la king, and chicken breast chunks into the hot oven. Stir everything well with a wooden spoon.

2. While the chicken and vegetables warm, sprinkle some flour on a cutting board and lay the unrolled sheets of pie crust dough side by side on the board. If only one pie crust will fit, work with one crust at a time.

3. Use a chef's knife to slice the pie crusts into long strips, each about 1 inch wide.

Servings: 11 to 13
Preparation Time—Total: 1 hour
Preparation Time—For the Scouts: 1 hour
Recommended Number of Chefs: 2 Scouts and 1 adult
Challenge Level: Easy

4. Carefully lay the dough strips next to each other, with gaps between them, over the hot meat and vegetables in the oven. When one row is finished, start a second row crosswise, like you'd see on a pie crust. Keep doing this until all the dough is used up.

5. Place the lid on the oven, then move 17 coals from under the oven to the lid.

6. Bake for about 30 to 35 minutes, until the crust is crisp.

7. Serve using a large serving spoon.

**Tim and Christine Conners, Statesboro, Georgia**
Committee Members and Merit Badge Counselors
Troop 340, Coastal Empire Council

**DANGER ZONE:**

- Hot coals! Enforce your fire-safe zone and use your gloves.

- Sharp utensils! Careful slicing required.

- Hot and heavy cookware! Use your gloves.

**HOT TIP!**
For fancier effect, the strips of pie dough can be woven together. Regardless of the method, perfect layering is not required, because it has no effect on the taste.

## Baden-Powell Barbecue Meatloaf

### INGREDIENTS
1 pound frozen mixed vegetables, your choice

1 pound lean ground beef

¼ cup dried minced onions

1 cup unseasoned dried breadcrumbs

2 eggs

1 (15- to18-ounce) bottle barbecue sauce

Salt and ground black pepper to taste

"Lord Baden-Powell was a famous British military leader who became the founder of the Boy Scouts. He understood that there were many lessons Scouts could learn while camping. In his words: 'A week of camp life is equal to six months of theoretical teaching in the meeting room.' Based upon your experiences at camp, what do you think Lord Baden-Powell meant by this? Ponder that as you enjoy your meatloaf!"

### REQUIRED EQUIPMENT:
12-inch camp Dutch oven
Briquettes and accessories for Dutch oven
Medium-size mixing bowl
Spatula

### INITIAL PREPARATION STEPS FOR ADULTS:
1. About an hour before starting the coals, set the mixed vegetables out to thaw if they are still frozen.

2. Prepare 25 briquettes for the Dutch oven.

3. About 45 minutes after starting the first batch of coals, begin a second batch of 25 coals.

### PREPARATION STEPS FOR YOUNG SCOUTS:
1. Put the ground beef into a medium-size bowl. Do this while an adult prepares the coals.

2. Pour the dried minced onions into the bowl, then add the breadcrumbs.

3. Crack the eggs into the bowl, then add ¼ cup of barbecue sauce.

4. Use clean hands to mush the ingredients in the bowl together until everything is evenly blended.

Servings: 6 to 8
Preparation Time—Total: 1 hour and 30 minutes
Preparation Time—For the Scouts: 30 minutes
Recommended Number of Chefs: 1 Scout and 1 adult
Challenge Level: Moderate

5. Form the meat mixture into a shape that resembles a small loaf of bread. Keep in mind that it will need to fit into the Dutch oven without touching the walls.

6. Set the meatloaf in the middle of the Dutch oven, keeping it away from the walls. Make sure that the loaf won't touch the inside of the lid once the lid is on the oven.

7. Pour the thawed vegetables around the sides of the meatloaf.

8. Once the adult says the coals are ready, put the lid on the oven, then set the oven on a metal tray. Place 8 coals under the oven and 17 coals on lid.

**FINAL PREPARATION STEPS FOR ADULTS:**

1. Take over the preparation from the Scouts, baking the meatloaf for about an hour, until the loaf is cooked through. The coals should be refreshed about 30 to 45 minutes after the lid goes on the oven.

2. Once off the coals, pour ¼ cup of barbecue sauce over the meatloaf. Add salt and black pepper to taste.

3. Slice the loaf with a spatula and serve with the vegetables. Any remaining barbecue sauce can be used as desired by the diners.

**Tim and Christine Conners, Statesboro, Georgia**
Committee Members and Merit Badge Counselors
Troop 340, Coastal Empire Council

**DANGER ZONE:**

- Hot coals! Enforce your fire-safe zone and use your gloves.
- Raw meat and eggs! Sanitize your hands after handling.
- Hot and heavy cookware! Use your gloves.

**HOT TIP!**
This classic meatloaf recipe uses raw ground beef and eggs that can cause food poisoning. Be sure not to cross-contaminate other items after handling the uncooked loaf!

# Tenderfoot Teriyaki Chicken

## INGREDIENTS

1 cup long grain rice

1 cup water

¼ teaspoon ground ginger

1 cup teriyaki baste and glaze

2 bell peppers

2 sweet onions

2 pounds skinless chicken breasts

1 (20-ounce) can pineapple chunks in heavy syrup

## REQUIRED EQUIPMENT:

12-inch camp Dutch oven
Briquettes and accessories for Dutch oven
Wooden spoon
Chef's knife
Can opener

## INITIAL PREPARATION STEPS FOR ADULTS:

1. Prepare 25 briquettes for the Dutch oven.

2. About 45 minutes after starting the first batch of coals, begin a second batch of 25.

3. Be prepared to show the Scouts how to chop bell peppers and onions into wedges.

## PREPARATION STEPS FOR YOUNG SCOUTS:

1. Pour the rice, the cup of water, the ground ginger, and the teriyaki baste and glaze sauce into the Dutch oven. Stir well with a wooden spoon. Do this step while an adult prepares the coals.

2. Remove the top stem-part from the bell peppers using a chef's knife. Next, cut the peppers in half, remove the seeds, then scrape out the white "ribs" on the inside. Cut the pieces in half again, from the top down, forming wedges.

3. Cut the stem and root part from the top and bottom of the onions, then peel off the dry skin. Also peel off the first layer of the onions under the dry skin.

4. Set the onions on the flat side where the stem or root part was removed. This will help keep it from rolling while you slice. Cut the onions from the top down, forming wedges.

5. Lay the chicken breasts over the rice, side by side, in the Dutch oven.

6. Cover the chicken breasts with the bell pepper and onion wedges.

Servings: 8 to 10
Preparation Time—Total: 1 hour and 30 minutes
Preparation Time—For the Scouts: 30 minutes
Recommended Number of Chefs: 2 Scouts and 1 adult
Challenge Level: Moderate

7. Pour the can of pineapple chunks, along with the syrup, over everything in the Dutch oven.

8. Once the adult says the coals are ready, put the lid on the oven, then set the oven on a metal tray. Place 8 coals under the oven and 17 coals on lid.

### FINAL PREPARATION STEP FOR ADULTS:

Take over the preparation from the Scouts, baking for about an hour, until the chicken is cooked through and the rice is tender. The coals should be refreshed about 30 to 45 minutes after the lid goes on the oven.

**Joseph Vanterpool, Statesboro, Georgia**
Eagle Scout
Troop 340, Coastal Empire Council

### DANGER ZONE:

- Hot coals! Enforce your fire-safe zone and use your gloves.

- Sharp utensils! Careful chopping required.

- Raw meat! Sanitize your hands after handling.

- Hot and heavy cookware! Use your gloves.

# Boulder Meatballs and Gravy

## INGREDIENTS
Vegetable oil for greasing Dutch oven

2 pounds lean ground beef

2 eggs

1 (5-ounce) can evaporated milk

1 tablespoon Original Blend Mrs. Dash seasoning

1 cup Italian-style bread crumbs

2 (10.75-ounce) cans condensed cream of mushroom soup

## REQUIRED EQUIPMENT:
12-inch camp Dutch oven
Briquettes and accessories for Dutch oven
Large mixing bowl
Can opener
Wooden spoon

## INITIAL PREPARATION STEPS FOR ADULTS:
1. Grease Dutch oven with a little vegetable oil.

2. Prepare 27 briquettes.

3. About 45 minutes after starting the first batch of coals, begin a second batch of 27.

## PREPARATION STEPS FOR YOUNG SCOUTS:
1. Place the ground beef in a large bowl, then crack the eggs over the raw meat. Do this while the adult prepares the coals.

2. Pour the can of evaporated milk over the eggs and meat.

3. Add the Mrs. Dash seasoning and the bread crumbs to the bowl.

4. Use a wooden spoon, or clean hands, to mix the ingredients completely together in the bowl.

5. Take a small amount of meat mixture from the bowl and compress it tightly between your hands to form a sphere about the size of a golf ball. Set the meatball in the Dutch oven.

6. Continue to form meatballs until all the meat is used. Fill the oven with one layer, then begin the next layer, and so on.

Servings: 9 to 11
Preparation Time—Total: 1 hour and 30 minutes
Preparation Time—For the Scouts: 1 hour
Recommended Number of Chefs: 3 Scouts and 1 adult
Challenge Level: Moderate

7. Once all the meatballs have been formed and placed in the oven, pour both cans of cream of mushroom soup over them. Don't stir the uncooked meatballs! If you do, they'll break apart.

8. Once the adult says the coals are ready, put the lid on the oven, then set the oven on a metal tray. Place 9 coals under the oven and 18 coals on lid.

9. About 30 minutes later, the coals should be mostly burned to ashes. Ask an adult for a new batch of hot coals, which should now be ready. Evenly spread 9 new coals under the oven and 18 new coals on lid.

## FINAL PREPARATION STEPS FOR ADULTS:

1. Take over the cooking from the Scouts after they set the new coals in place.

2. Continue baking for about 30 more minutes, until meatballs are cooked through.

**Beverly Jo Antonini, Morgantown, West Virginia**
Assistant Scoutmaster
Troop 49, Mountaineer Area Council

**DANGER ZONE:**

• Hot coals! Enforce your fire-safe zone and use your gloves.

• Raw meat and eggs! Sanitize your hands after handling.

• Hot and heavy cookware! Use your gloves.

**HOT TIP!**
A tablespoon can be used to scoop out globs of meat from the bowl to form meatballs with a more consistent size.

## INGREDIENTS

2 tablespoons vegetable oil

1 pound small red potatoes

1 pound sweet potatoes

6 boneless chicken breast halves

2 (12-ounce) jars turkey gravy

2 (6-ounce) packages Stove Top stuffing mix for turkey

2 (14.75-ounce) cans cream style sweet corn

2 (14-ounce) cans whole berry cranberry sauce

# Thanksgiving at Camp

"Enjoy a classic Thanksgiving meal in the woods. The only thing missing is the football game!"

## REQUIRED EQUIPMENT:

12-inch camp Dutch oven
Briquettes and accessories for Dutch oven
Chef's knife
Potato peeler
Can opener
Serving spoon

## INITIAL PREPARATION STEPS FOR ADULTS:

1. Prepare 25 briquettes for the Dutch oven.

2. About 45 minutes after starting the first batch of coals, begin a second batch of 25.

## PREPARATION STEPS FOR YOUNG SCOUTS:

1. Pour the vegetable oil into the Dutch oven. Do this while an adult prepares the coals.

2. Wash the red potatoes and the sweet potatoes, if they haven't been washed already.

3. Slice the red potatoes about ¼ to ½ inch thick (about the thickness of your finger) using a chef's knife. Lay the potato slices evenly over the bottom of the oven.

4. Peel the skin from the sweet potatoes using a potato peeler, then slice the sweet potatoes the same way as the red potatoes, but don't place the sweet potato slices in the oven just yet.

5. Slice in half each of chicken breast halves, then set the twelve pieces evenly over the potatoes in the Dutch oven.

6. Pour both jars of turkey gravy over the chicken and potatoes in the Dutch oven.

Servings: 12
Preparation Time—Total: 1 hour and 30 minutes
Preparation Time—For the Scouts: 30 minutes
Recommended Number of Chefs: 3 Scouts and 1 adult
Challenge Level: Moderate

7. Sprinkle the packages of stuffing mix over the gravy.

8. Pour the cans of creamed corn over the stuffing mix.

9. Lay the slices of sweet potatoes evenly over the creamed corn.

10. Finally, spoon the cranberry sauce over the sweet potatoes.

11. Once the adult says the coals are ready, put the lid on the oven, then set the oven on a metal tray. Place 8 coals under the oven and 17 coals on lid.

## FINAL PREPARATION STEPS FOR ADULTS:

1. Take over the preparation from the Scouts, baking for about an hour, until the chicken is cooked through, the sweet potatoes are tender, and the cranberries are bubbling. The coals will need to be refreshed about 30 minutes after the lid goes on the oven.

2. Serve, scooping through to the bottom with a serving spoon so that everyone gets some of all the layers.

**Tom Hoops, Edison, New Jersey**
Committee Member
Troop 66, Central New Jersey Council

**DANGER ZONE:**

- Hot coals! Enforce your fire-safe zone and use your gloves.
- Sharp utensils! Careful chopping required.
- Raw meat! Sanitize your hands after handling.
- Hot and heavy cookware! Use your gloves.

**HOT TIP!**
Picky Scouts may not like the sweet potatoes and cranberry sauce. If this is the case for your troop, these items can be left out. Simply stop layering after adding the creamed corn.

# Orange Chicken

## INGREDIENTS

2 (6.2-ounce) packages Uncle Ben's long grain and wild rice

4½ cups water

1 (15-ounce) can sweet peas

2 pounds uncooked boneless chicken tenderloins

1 (18-ounce) jar orange marmalade

### DANGER ZONE:

• Hot coals! Enforce your fire-safe zone and use your gloves.

• Raw meat! Sanitize your hands after handling.

• Hot and heavy cookware! Use your gloves.

## REQUIRED EQUIPMENT:

12-inch camp Dutch oven
Briquettes and accessories for Dutch oven
Wooden spoon
Can opener

## INITIAL PREPARATION STEPS FOR ADULTS:

1. Prepare 25 briquettes for the Dutch oven.

2. About 45 minutes after starting the first batch of coals, begin a second batch of 25.

## PREPARATION STEPS FOR YOUNG SCOUTS:

1. Dump both packages of long grain and wild rice into the Dutch oven. Also add the contents of the seasoning packets found in the boxes of rice. Do this while an adult prepares the coals.

2. Pour the 4½ cups of water into the oven and stir with a wooden spoon.

3. Drain the juice from the can of peas and pour the peas over the rice. Mix again with the spoon.

4. Lay the chicken tenderloins side by side over the rice and peas in the oven.

5. Spoon the orange marmalade over the top of the chicken.

6. Once the adult says the coals are ready, put the lid on the oven, then set the oven on a metal tray. Place 8 coals under the oven and 17 coals on lid.

## FINAL PREPARATION STEP FOR ADULTS:

Take over the preparation from the Scouts, baking for 1½ hours until the chicken is cooked through and the liquid has been fully absorbed by the rice. The coals will need to be refreshed about 45 minutes after the lid goes on the oven.

**Donna Pettigrew, Anderson, Indiana**
Tanglewood Camp Director and
Master Trainer
Girl Scouts of Central Indiana

Servings: 10 to 12
Preparation Time—Total: 1 hour and 45 minutes
Preparation Time—For the Scouts: 15 minutes
Recommended Number of Chefs: 1 Scout and 1 adult
Challenge Level: Easy

# Troll Stew

## REQUIRED EQUIPMENT:
12-inch camp Dutch oven
Briquettes and accessories for Dutch oven
Chef's knife
Gallon-size ziplock bag
Can opener
Wooden spoon

## INITIAL PREPARATION STEPS FOR ADULTS:
1. About an hour before starting the coals, set the frozen vegetables out to thaw if they haven't already.

2. Prepare 25 briquettes for the Dutch oven.

3. Pour vegetable oil into oven and warm over all 25 coals on a metal tray.

4. About 45 minutes after starting the first batch of coals, begin a second batch of 12.

## PREPARATION STEPS FOR YOUNG SCOUTS:
1. Trim any large areas of fat from the stew meat using a chef's knife, then cut the meat into bite-size cubes. Do this while the adult prepares the Dutch oven.

2. Pour the cup of flour into a large ziplock bag and add the cubes of meat to the bag.

3. Seal the ziplock bag shut. Double-check that it's tightly closed, then hold the bag with two hands on the seal and shake it until all the beef cubes are covered in flour.

4. Once the adult says the Dutch oven is ready, very carefully add the stew meat to the hot oil in the Dutch oven. Leave any unused flour in the bag.

5. Using the wooden spoon to turn the cubes, cook the meat until all sides of the beef are browned. This will take about 5 minutes. Don't cook the meat all the way through on this step. It isn't necessary.

## INGREDIENTS
3 (16-ounce) packages Bird's Eye Recipe Ready Stew Blend frozen vegetables

⅓ cup vegetable oil

2 pounds beef stew meat, such as chuck, round, or rump

1 cup all-purpose flour

2 (32-ounce) cartons beef broth

1 (6-ounce) can tomato paste

**HOT TIP!**
If Bird's Eye Recipe Ready vegetables are unavailable, a blend of frozen carrots, onions, potatoes, and celery can be mixed by hand instead.

Servings: 12 to 14
Preparation Time—Total: 1 hour and 45 minutes
Preparation Time—For the Scouts: 1 hour
Recommended Number of Chefs: 1 Scout and 1 adult
Challenge Level: Moderate

6. Pour both containers of broth into the oven, then scoop the tomato paste into it. Stir everything together.

7. Cut the number of coals under the oven in half to reduce the heat, then place the lid on the oven. No coals go on the lid.

8. About 30 minutes later, the coals should be mostly burned to ashes and will need to be replaced. Ask an adult for a batch of new, hot coals, which should now be ready. Evenly spread 12 new coals under the oven.

## FINAL PREPARATION STEPS FOR ADULTS:

1. Take over the cooking from the Scouts after they set the new coals in place.

2. Continue baking for another 30 minutes, then remove the lid and add the stew vegetables to the oven. Stir everything well.

3. Cover and bake for an additional 15 minutes or until the vegetables become tender.

**Tim and Christine Conners, Statesboro, Georgia**
Committee Members and Merit Badge Counselors
Troop 340, Coastal Empire Council

Is it made from trolls, or is it a meal that trolls would love? You be the judge. One thing's for sure—it tastes fantastic. *Christine Conners*

# Klondike Derby Baked Ziti

"When the troop needed someone to supply a meal for almost twenty Scouts and leaders during a Klondike Derby a few years ago, I volunteered to cook this recipe. People thought I was crazy as I poured uncooked ziti into the Dutch oven, but it came out great. The temperature dropped to 15 degrees that day, so everyone was glad to have a hot meal in them."

## REQUIRED EQUIPMENT:
12-inch camp Dutch oven
Briquettes and accessories for Dutch oven
Wooden spoon

## INITIAL PREPARATION STEPS FOR ADULTS:
1. Prepare 25 briquettes for the Dutch oven.

2. Warm the oven over all 25 coals on a metal tray.

3. About 45 minutes after starting the first batch of coals, begin a second batch of 25.

## PREPARATION STEPS FOR YOUNG SCOUTS:
1. Once the adult says the Dutch oven is ready to use, add the ground beef to the hot oven. Break up the lumps of meat with a wooden spoon while the beef cooks.

2. Stir the beef often while it browns until there is no sign of pink left in the meat.

3. Add the ziti pasta to the oven, then pour all four jars of spaghetti sauce over the beef and pasta. Stir until all the noodles are covered in sauce.

4. Place the lid on the oven, then move 17 of the coals from under the oven to the lid. Make sure all the coals are evenly spread on the lid and underneath.

5. About 30 minutes later, the coals should be mostly burned to ashes and will need to be replaced. Ask an adult for a batch of new, hot coals, which should now be ready. Evenly spread 17 coals on the lid and 8 under the oven.

### INGREDIENTS
**1 pound lean ground beef**

**1 (16-ounce) package ziti pasta**

**4 (26-ounce) jars spaghetti sauce**

**1 (15-ounce) container ricotta cheese**

**1 (16-ounce) package shredded mozzarella cheese**

Servings: 13 to 15
Preparation Time—Total: 2 hours
Preparation Time—For the Scouts: 1 hour
Recommended Number of Chefs: 1 Scout and 1 adult
Challenge Level: Moderate

# DINNER

**HOT TIP!** The final step for the Scouts can be taken over by the adults, if desired. But the purpose of this step is to teach the Scouts to carefully watch the clock when cooking.

**FINAL PREPARATION STEPS FOR ADULTS:**

1. Take over the cooking from the Scouts after they set the new coals in place.

2. Continue baking for another 30 minutes, then remove the lid and add the ricotta cheese and shredded mozzarella cheese to the oven. Stir everything well.

3. Cover and bake for an additional 20 minutes or until the pasta is soft.

**Tom Hoops, Edison, New Jersey**
Committee Member
Troop 66, Central New Jersey Council

# Girl Scout Stew

"This recipe brings back so many great memories of Scout camp. I brought home dirty clothes, a burn on my finger (from preparing this stew), and memories I'll cherish forever."

## REQUIRED EQUIPMENT:
Cookstove
Large cook pot
Wooden spoon
Can opener
Ladle

## INITIAL PREPARATION STEP FOR ADULTS:
Prepare cookstove.

## PREPARATION STEPS FOR YOUNG SCOUTS:

1. Put the ground beef into the cook pot. Place the pot on the stove, light the flame, then set the heat halfway between low and high.

2. Use a wooden spoon to constantly stir and break up the chunks of meat. Cook until the meat is no longer pink. If the beef begins to burn, lower the flame.

3. Pour all the cans of tomato soup and alphabet soup into the pot.

4. Add the can of mixed vegetables, including the juice, to the pot.

5. Stir the stew well using the wooden spoon, then set the flame to low.

6. Occasionally stir the stew until it is hot, then turn off the stove.

7. Serve the stew with a ladle.

**Kathleen Kirby, Milltown, New Jersey**
Merit Badge Counselor
Troop 33, Central New Jersey Council

## INGREDIENTS
**2 pounds lean ground beef**

**2 (10.75-ounce) cans condensed tomato soup**

**4 (10.75-ounce) cans condensed alphabet soup**

**1 (15-ounce) can mixed vegetables**

### HOT TIP!
Young Scouts should always ask adults for help if hot and heavy cookware needs to be moved, even when wearing barbecue gloves or using hot pads to protect hands and arms.

### DANGER ZONE:
• Raw meat! Sanitize your hands after handling.

• Hot and heavy cookware! Be careful not to spill contents.

Servings: 15 to 17
Preparation Time—Total: 30 minutes
Preparation Time—For the Scouts: 30 minutes
Recommended Number of Chefs: 1 Scout and 1 adult
Challenge Level: Easy

## Colonel Barrett's Ozark Rice Dinner

**INGREDIENTS**

1¾ cups water

1 (6.2-ounce) package Uncle Ben's Fast Cook long grain and wild rice

1 bunch green onions

1 (14-ounce) package "smokies" smoked sausage

1 (14.5-ounce) can diced tomatoes

1 (15-ounce) can seasoned black beans

"I am the descendant of some very colorful ancestors who settled Kentucky, Illinois, and Missouri. The Barrett family were early pioneers. Colonel John Stephen Barrett, for whom this recipe is named, was a member of Missouri's first legislature. He was also a doctor and Methodist-Episcopal minister. The Colonel's family served in the Revolutionary War, the War of 1812, the battle of San Juan Hill, and the Civil War. Do you have any stories about your ancestors you can share around the campfire?"

**REQUIRED EQUIPMENT:**
Cookstove
Medium-size cook pot with lid
Wooden spoon
Can opener
Chef's knife

**INITIAL PREPARATION STEP FOR ADULTS:**
Prepare cookstove.

**PREPARATION STEPS FOR YOUNG SCOUTS:**

1. Place the 1¾ cups of water in a medium-size cook pot.

2. Pour the rice from the Uncle Ben's package into the water, then tear open the rice seasoning packet and add its contents to the water too. Stir with a wooden spoon.

3. Place the pot on the stove and set the heat to high.

4. Once the water begins to boil hard, reduce the flame until the water is just barely boiling. Stir the rice again, then put the lid on the pot.

5. Cook the rice for 5 minutes, then turn the heat off. Leave the lid on for now.

Servings: 5 to 7
Preparation Time—Total: 45 minutes
Preparation Time—For the Scouts: 45 minutes
Recommended Number of Chefs: 2 Scouts and 1 adult
Challenge Level: Moderate

6. Cut the ragged top parts from all the green onions and throw the ragged pieces away. Remove the stringy roots too. Chop the rest of the onions into pieces.

7. Chop each of the smokies into three pieces.

8. Add the chopped green onions and smokies to the pot with the rice.

9. Open the cans of tomatoes and beans but don't drain the juices. Pour the tomatoes and beans, along with their juices, into the pot.

10. Stir the bean and rice mix well. Turn the stove back on to a low flame and warm the mixture for a few minutes. Stir occasionally to keep the rice and beans from burning.

11. Turn off the stove.

**Howard Fisk, Springfield, Missouri**
Committee Chair
Troop 1, Ozark Trails Council

**DANGER ZONE:**

- Sharp utensils! Careful chopping required.
- Hot pot! Turn the handle inward and be careful not to spill contents.

**HOT TIP!**
There are a couple of tricks to making a good batch of rice. First, don't cook with a strong boil. Instead, use a gentle simmer. Second, don't take the lid off while the rice is cooking.

Any recipe named for a famous guy AND a mountain range must be good! *Christine Conners*

# Order of the Arrow Cheesy Pasta

"I prepare this for my Order of the Arrow boys on Friday evenings."

## INGREDIENTS

4 cups milk

2 tablespoons cornstarch

½ teaspoon salt

1 (16-ounce) package rotini pasta

16 ounces shredded Italian blend cheese

8 ounces shredded sharp cheddar cheese

¼ cup (½ standard stick) butter

## REQUIRED EQUIPMENT:
Cookstove
Large cook pot
Medium-size mixing bowl
Long-handled wooden spoon

## INITIAL PREPARATION STEPS FOR ADULTS:
1. Prepare cookstove.

2. Fill a large pot halfway full with water and bring it to a boil.

3. Be ready to help the Scouts drain hot water from the pasta once it's ready.

## PREPARATION STEPS FOR YOUNG SCOUTS:
1. Pour the milk into a medium-size bowl, then add the cornstarch and salt to the milk in the bowl. Stir well with a wooden spoon until the lumps are gone. Do this while the adult prepares the boiling water.

2. Add the rotini noodles to the boiling water and stir for a few seconds with the wooden spoon.

3. Allow the noodles to boil until they become soft and tender. This will take about 10 minutes. Occasionally taste the noodles to see if they're done.

4. Turn off the stove, then ask an adult to help with draining the hot water from the pasta. Do not do this yourself!

5. Once the water is drained, place the pot with the pasta in it back on the stove. If the pot is still too heavy, ask an adult for help!

Servings: 6 to 8
Preparation Time—Total: 45 minutes
Preparation Time—For the Scouts: 45 minutes
Recommended Number of Chefs: 1 Scout and 1 adult
Challenge Level: Moderate

6. Pour the milk mixture from the bowl into the pot with the pasta.

7. Add the shredded Italian blend cheese and shredded cheddar cheese to the pot of pasta.

8. Drop the half-stick of butter into the pot. Mix all the ingredients well.

9. Turn the stove back on and set it to a low flame. Warm the pasta until the cheese and butter melt. Stir the pasta often to keep it from burning.

10. Turn off the stove.

**FINAL PREPARATION STEP FOR ADULTS:**
Help the Scouts move the hot pot of pasta to the serving area once it's ready.

**Beverly Jo Antonini, Morgantown, West Virginia**
Assistant Scoutmaster
Troop 49, Mountaineer Area Council

**DANGER ZONE:**
- Boiling water! An adult must drain large pots.
- Hot and heavy cookware! Be careful not to spill contents.

*HOT TIP!*
Don't overcook any type of pasta, or it will turn mushy and waterlogged.

## Leprechaun Garden Pasta

"When leprechauns aren't busy making shoes, playing tricks, or hiding gold at the end of the rainbow, you can find them tending to their vegetables in their secret gardens. Here's one of their favorite recipes. And if you like pasta primavera, it will become one of yours, too!"

### INGREDIENTS

1 cup (2 standard sticks) butter

2 pounds frozen vegetable blend, your choice

2 pounds fettuccine pasta

2 cups heavy cream

2 cups grated Parmesan cheese

1 teaspoon salt

1 teaspoon ground black pepper

### REQUIRED EQUIPMENT:
Cookstove
Large cook pot
Long-handled wooden spoon

### INITIAL PREPARATION STEPS FOR ADULTS:

1. Set butter and frozen vegetables in a warm location to soften about an hour before dinner.

2. Prepare cookstove once it's time to cook.

3. Fill a large pot halfway full with water and set it on the stove over high flame.

4. When it comes time for the Scouts to cook the pasta, keep a close eye to be certain the pot and its hot water are never at risk of tipping. If Scouts have trouble managing the pot in any way, take over this step from them! Be ready to drain the hot water from the pot when the pasta is done.

### PREPARATION STEPS FOR YOUNG SCOUTS:

1. Once the water in the pot comes to a boil, break the fettuccine noodles in half and carefully drop them into the hot water. Immediately stir the noodles well with a long wooden spoon.

2. Cook the pasta for about 10 to 12 minutes, stirring occasionally, until the noodles are tender. Don't overcook them, or they'll turn mushy. Carefully sample the noodles after about 10 minutes to see if they're ready.

3. Once the noodles are ready, turn off the stove.

### DANGER ZONE:

- Boiling water! An adult must drain large pots.

- Hot and heavy cookware! Be careful not to spill contents.

Servings: 13 to 15
Preparation Time—Total: 45 minutes
Preparation Time—For the Scouts: 45 minutes
Recommended Number of Chefs: 1 Scout and 1 adult
Challenge Level: Moderate

4. Ask an adult to completely drain the hot water from the pot but to leave the noodles in the pot. Be sure that they return the pot to the stove.

5. Drop the sticks of softened butter into the pot with the noodles. Stir well with the wooden spoon until the butter melts, then add the heavy cream. Stir again.

6. Pour the grated parmesan cheese into the pot along with the salt and pepper. Stir everything well.

7. Turn the stove back on to a low setting.

8. Add the thawed vegetables to the pot and stir again. Continue to cook over low heat until the vegetables are heated through.

9. Turn off the stove, then serve the pasta.

**Tim and Christine Conners, Statesboro, Georgia**
Committee Members and Merit Badge Counselors
Troop 340, Coastal Empire Council

### Chef's Corner

You may wonder why you need to stir noodles in boiling water when it seems like the churning water is doing the job for you. When you first drop dry pasta into hot water, the noodles will always want to immediately stick together. In fact, if you wait too long, it becomes nearly impossible to separate them!

We normally try to keep the leprechauns out of the pasta, but we made an exception with this recipe.
*Christine Conners*

# Chickasaw Cajun Corn

"This recipe is a big hit with our Scouts!"

## INGREDIENTS

1 cup water

1 (12-count) package frozen half-ears corn on the cob

1 pound small red-skin potatoes

2 pounds smoked sausage links

1 large onion

1 (16-ounce) package baby carrots

1 small head cabbage

1 teaspoon Cajun seasoning

## REQUIRED EQUIPMENT:

Cookstove
Large cook pot with lid
Chef's knife
Large serving tray

## INITIAL PREPARATION STEPS FOR ADULTS:

1. Prepare cookstove.

2. Set a large pot on the stove.

## PREPARATION STEPS FOR YOUNG SCOUTS:

1. Pour the cup of water into the pot on the stove. Do not turn on the stove yet!

2. Set the half-ears of corn in the bottom of the pot so that the ears are all standing vertically.

3. Use a chef's knife to cut the potatoes into bite-size pieces. Do the same to the smoked sausages. Set the potato and sausage chunks in the pot over and around the corn.

4. Use a chef's knife to cut the stem and root part from the top and bottom of the onion, then peel off the dry skin.

5. Set the onion on a flat end where the stem or root part was removed to keep it from rolling, then chop it into bite-size chunks. Place the onion pieces in the pot.

6. Lay the baby carrots over all the ingredients in the pot.

7. Cut the ragged outer leaves from a small head of cabbage and throw them away. Tear the remaining leaves from the cabbage and rip them into smaller pieces with clean hands. Place the cabbage pieces over the carrots in the pot.

8. Set the stove to a medium flame, about halfway between the lowest and highest settings. Cover the pot with a lid.

Servings: 10 to 12
Preparation Time—Total: 60 minutes
Preparation Time—For the Scouts: 30 minutes
Recommended Number of Chefs: 3 Scouts and 1 adult
Challenge Level: Easy

## FINAL PREPARATION STEPS FOR ADULTS:

1. Take over the cooking from the Scouts after the lid goes on the pot.

2. Cook for about 30 minutes, until potatoes become soft.

3. Drain liquid from the pot, then pour the pot's contents onto a large serving tray.

4. Sprinkle the food with Cajun seasoning and serve.

**Darlene Griffith, Tunica, Mississippi**
Committee Chairperson
Troop 16, Chickasaw Council

Chickasaw Cajun Corn has tremendous flavor and is easy to prepare. *Christine Conners*

## Salmon Stew

"This is a simple but delicious recipe that comes from the family of my wife, Janie."

**INGREDIENTS**

6 small red-skin potatoes

2 (14.75-ounce) cans salmon

2 tablespoons butter (about ¼ standard stick)

2 (12-ounce) cans evaporated milk

14¾ ounces milk (to fill an empty salmon can)

14¾ ounces water (to fill an empty salmon can)

Salt and ground black pepper to taste

**REQUIRED EQUIPMENT:**
Cookstove
Chef's knife
Can opener
Medium-size cook pot
Wooden spoon

**INITIAL PREPARATION STEP FOR ADULTS:**
Prepare cookstove.

**PREPARATION STEPS FOR YOUNG SCOUTS:**

1. Chop the potatoes into small pieces with a chef's knife.

2. Empty the cans of salmon, along with their juice, into a cook pot.

3. Drop butter into the pot. Bring flame to a high setting.

4. Once the butter melts, stir gently while cooking the salmon for about 1 minute.

5. Add the chopped potatoes to the pot along with both cans of evaporated milk.

6. Fill one of the empty salmon cans to the top with milk, then pour it into the pot.

7. Now fill the empty salmon can to the top with water, then add it to the pot too.

8. Stir all the ingredients well, then reduce the flame until the stew barely boils.

**FINAL PREPARATION STEPS FOR ADULTS:**

1. Take over the cooking and keep an eye on the stew, stirring occasionally for about 1 hour.

2. When ready to serve, add salt and black pepper to taste.

**DANGER ZONE:**

- Sharp utensils! Careful chopping required.

- Hot pot! Turn the handle inward and be careful not to spill contents.

Servings: 8 to 10
Preparation Time—Total: 1 hour and 15 minutes
Preparation Time—For the Scouts: 15 minutes
Recommended Number of Chefs: 2 Scouts and 1 adult
Challenge Level: Easy

Jeff Edgens, Augusta, Georgia
Eagle Scout
Troop 91, Northwest Georgia Council

# Menehune Pork with Pineapple

"Hawaiian legend says that deep in the wet, dark forests of Hawaii live a mischievous people called the Menehunes. They stand only two feet tall. Despite their size, the Menehunes are rumored to have superhuman strength. If you ever camp in Hawaii, keep your eyes and ears open, because they play tricks on people during the night. And while you're losing sleep, enjoy this recipe inspired by the luaus of Hawaii!"

**INGREDIENTS**

2 pounds thick-sliced smoked ham

8 teaspoons brown sugar

1 (20-ounce) can sliced pineapple

1 (10-ounce) jar maraschino cherries

**REQUIRED EQUIPMENT:**
Heavy-duty aluminum foil
Can opener
Long-handled tongs

**INITIAL PREPARATION STEP FOR ADULTS:**
Prepare a wood fire well in advance of mealtime, giving the fire time to die down to a low bed of embers.

**PREPARATION STEPS FOR YOUNG SCOUTS:**

1. Tear off eight sheets of aluminum foil. Each sheet of foil should be at least three times larger than a slice of the ham.

2. Place a ham slice on each of the sheets of foil. Each slice of ham should be placed near one end of its foil sheet because of the way in which the foil will eventually be wrapped. Repeat doing this, stacking the ham on each sheet of foil until all the ham is used up.

3. Sprinkle 1 teaspoon of brown sugar over each stack of ham, for 8 teaspoons total.

4. Open the can of pineapple and lay a pineapple ring over each stack of ham.

5. Set a cherry in the middle of each pineapple ring.

> **HOT TIP!**
> Seal your foil packets tightly. The moisture will then stay trapped in the pouch and help keep the ham from drying out and burning.

> Servings: 8
> Preparation Time—Total: 1 hour and 30 minutes (including 1 hour to prepare the fire)
> Preparation Time—For the Scouts: 30 minutes
> Recommended Number of Chefs: 2 Scouts and 1 adult
> Challenge Level: Easy

6. Wrap each ham stack in the foil. Bring the empty half of the foil over the top of the ham stack, then fold each of the three open edges over on itself several times for a tight seal. If you have trouble understanding this step, ask an adult for help. Once finished, you'll have eight foil packets.

7. Lay each packet directly on the embers in the fire using long-handled tongs.

8. Heat for 3 to 5 minutes, then flip the packets and heat for another 3 to 5 minutes.

9. Remove the packets from the fire and allow them to cool for a few minutes.

### FINAL PREPARATION STEP FOR ADULTS:

Steam burns are possible when opening foil packets if caution isn't used. Help the Scouts open their packets, making sure that they give their food a few minutes to cool off before doing so.

**Tim and Christine Conners, Statesboro, Georgia**
Committee Members and Merit Badge Counselors
Troop 340, Coastal Empire Council

Menehune Pork with Pineapple, before sealing in foil. *Christine Conners*

And here it is after sealing tightly. *Christine Conners*

# Hidden Chili Dogs

**REQUIRED EQUIPMENT:**
Folding camp grill (if fire pit doesn't have a grate)
Heavy-duty aluminum foil
Can opener
Long-handled tongs

**INITIAL PREPARATION STEPS FOR ADULTS:**

1. Prepare a wood fire well in advance of mealtime, giving the fire time to die down to a low bed of embers.

2. Move the fire pit's grill grate into position over the fire. If the fire pit doesn't have a built-in grate, set up a folding camp grill over the embers.

**PREPARATION STEPS FOR YOUNG SCOUTS:**

1. Cut ten sheets of aluminum foil, each about 8 to 10 inches long. The size doesn't need to be exact, but the sheets need to be larger than the tortillas. Spread out all the sheets of foil on a clean surface.

2. Place a tortilla in the center of each sheet of foil.

3. Set a hot dog in the center of each tortilla.

4. Top each of the hot dogs with some chili and cheese. Use up all the chili and cheese and try to divide them evenly on top of all the hot dogs.

5. Roll up each tortilla, then wrap each rolled tortilla in its foil sheet. Be sure that extra foil remains on either end of the tortilla, then twist the foil on the ends so that the tortilla is sealed shut.

6. Use tongs to place the foil packets on a grill grate over the embers in the fire.

7. Allow the packets to heat for about 10 minutes.

8. Remove the packets from the fire and allow them to cool for a few minutes.

**INGREDIENTS**

10 (6-inch) flour tortillas

10 regular-size hot dogs

1 (15-ounce) can chili with beans

1 (8-ounce) package shredded Mexican blend cheese

Optional: chopped lettuce and tomato

**HOT TIP!**
This recipe can also be cooked on a regular charcoal or gas grill.

Servings: 10
Preparation Time—Total: 1 hour and 30 minutes
(including 1 hour to prepare the fire)
Preparation Time—For the Scouts: 30 minutes
Recommended Number of Chefs: 2 Scouts and 1 adult
Challenge Level: Easy

## Chef's Corner

Cooking in foil isn't difficult when the packets are placed on a grate, as in this recipe. But it's more challenging when the packets are set directly in the embers, like when using potatoes or cuts of meat, because it's easier to overcook or undercook the food.

## DANGER ZONE:

- Live fire! Use barbecue gloves while working with a wood fire.

- Hot steam! Use care to avoid burns when opening foil packets.

## FINAL PREPARATION STEPS FOR ADULTS:

1. Steam burns are possible when opening foil packets if caution isn't used. Help the Scouts open their packets, making sure they give their food a few minutes to cool off before doing so.

2. Have the Scouts add optional lettuce and tomato to taste.

**Donna Pettigrew, Anderson, Indiana**
Tanglewood Camp Director and Master Trainer
Girl Scouts of Central Indiana

# Adventurer's Veggie Soup

"A veggie soup young adventurers will love!"

**REQUIRED EQUIPMENT:**
12-inch camp Dutch oven
Briquettes and accessories for Dutch oven
Chef's knife
Wooden spoon
Can opener
Ladle

**INITIAL PREPARATION STEPS FOR ADULTS:**
1. Prepare 25 briquettes for the Dutch oven.
2. Pour the vegetable oil into the oven.
3. Warm the oven over all 25 coals on a metal tray.

**PREPARATION STEPS FOR YOUNG SCOUTS:**
1. Slice the leafy part from the stalks of celery using a chef's knife, then cut off the wide, white bottom part from each stalk. You should have about 6 to 8 inches of usable stalk left for each. Do this while the adult prepares the Dutch oven.
2. Cut the celery into thin slices, then chop the slices into small pieces.
3. Slice the stem and root from the top and bottom of the onion, then peel off the dry skin.
4. Set the onion on a flat end where the stem or root part was removed to keep it from rolling, then chop it into small pieces.
5. Slice the stem end from both zucchini, then cut each of the zucchini into slices about as thick as one of your fingers. Chop the slices into small pieces.
6. Add the chopped celery, onion, and zucchini to the Dutch oven once the adult says it's ready.

**INGREDIENTS**
2 tablespoons vegetable oil
2 stalks celery
1 medium-size onion
2 medium-size zucchini
1 (11-ounce) can Green Giant Mexicorn
1 (32-ounce) carton vegetable broth
1 (15-ounce) can tomato sauce
½ cup instant rice

Servings: 14 to 16
Preparation Time—Total: 1 hour
Preparation Time—For the Scouts: 1 hour
Recommended Number of Chefs: 2 Scouts and 1 adult
Challenge Level: Moderate

7. Fry the vegetables until they become soft. This will take about 10 minutes. Use a wooden spoon to occasionally stir them while they're frying.

8. Add the Mexicorn, the vegetable broth, the tomato sauce, and the instant rice to the Dutch oven. Stir everything well.

9. Once the soup begins to boil, remove about 5 of the coals from under the oven to reduce the heat. Wait a few minutes. If the soup continues to boil, remove more coals gradually until it stops.

10. Stir occasionally and continue to simmer the soup for about 15 minutes before serving using a ladle.

**Ken Harbison, Rochester, New York**
Former Boy Scout
Washington Trails Council

### DANGER ZONE:

- Hot coals! Enforce your fire-safe zone and use your gloves.

- Sharp utensils! Careful chopping required.

- Hot and heavy cookware! Use your gloves.

# Coyote Corn Casserole

"This recipe will make your taste buds howl!"

## REQUIRED EQUIPMENT:
12-inch camp Dutch oven
Briquettes and accessories for Dutch oven
Large mixing bowl
Can opener
Wooden spoon

## INITIAL PREPARATION STEPS FOR ADULTS:
1. About an hour before starting the coals, set a stick of butter in a warm location to soften.

2. Prepare 25 briquettes for the Dutch oven.

## PREPARATION STEPS FOR YOUNG SCOUTS:
1. Crack the eggs into a large bowl, then mix them by stirring very quickly with a fork. Do this while an adult prepares the coals for the Dutch oven.

2. Add the can of whole kernel corn, including its juice, and the can of creamed corn to the bowl with the eggs. Drop the softened stick of butter into the bowl.

3. Pour the contents of the package of corn muffin mix into the bowl along with the sour cream. Stir all the ingredients together with a wooden spoon.

4. Spray the inside of the Dutch oven with cooking spray, then pour the batter into the oven.

## FINAL PREPARATION STEP FOR ADULTS:
Bake for 45 minutes to 1 hour or until the top becomes golden and a knife or toothpick inserted into the cornbread comes out clean. Depending on how long it takes the Scouts to prepare the batter, a refreshing of the coals may be required.

**Carl Laub, Arlington Heights, Illinois**
Executive Board Member
Northwest Suburban Council

## INGREDIENTS
½ cup (1 standard stick) butter

2 eggs

1 (15-ounce) can whole kernel corn

1 (15-ounce) can creamed corn

1 (8.5-ounce) package Jiffy corn muffin mix

1 (8-ounce) container sour cream

Cooking spray

### DANGER ZONE:
- Hot coals! Enforce your fire-safe zone and use your gloves.
- Raw eggs! Sanitize your hands after handling.
- Hot and heavy cookware! Use your gloves.

Servings: 10 to 12
Preparation Time—Total: 1 hour and 15 minutes
Preparation Time—For the Scouts: 30 minutes
Recommended Number of Chefs: 1 Scout and 1 adult
Challenge Level: Moderate

# Wild Whistle-Berry Beans

"Named for the many 'whistles' heard after this dish is served!"

**INGREDIENTS**

2 large onions

1 pound ground pork sausage

2 (53-ounce) cans pork and beans

1 cup brown sugar

½ cup ketchup

½ cup barbecue sauce

3 tablespoons prepared (yellow) mustard

½ teaspoon chili powder

**REQUIRED EQUIPMENT:**
12-inch camp Dutch oven
Briquettes and accessories for Dutch oven
Chef's knife
Wooden spoon
Can opener

**INITIAL PREPARATION STEPS FOR ADULTS:**

1. Prepare 25 briquettes for the Dutch oven.

2. Warm the oven over all 25 coals on a metal tray.

3. About 45 minutes after starting the first batch of coals, begin a second batch of 12 coals.

**PREPARATION STEPS FOR YOUNG SCOUTS:**

1. Cut the stem and root part from the top and bottom of the onions, then peel off the dry skin. Do this while an adult prepares the Dutch oven.

2. Set the onions on a flat end where the stem or root part was removed to keep them from rolling, then chop them into small pieces. Place the chopped onions in the Dutch oven once the adult says it's ready to use.

3. Add the pork sausage to the oven. Break the lumps of sausage apart using a wooden spoon. Stir the onions and sausage together.

4. Continue to stir until the onions have bits of brown on them. It's okay if the meat isn't fully cooked, because in a later step it will be.

Servings: 20 to 24
Preparation Time—Total: 1 hour and 45 minutes
Preparation Time—For the Scouts: 45 minutes
Recommended Number of Chefs: 2 Scouts and 1 adult
Challenge Level: Moderate

5. Open the two cans of pork and beans and drain out about half of the juice from each can, then add the pork and beans and remaining juice to the Dutch oven.

6. Pour the brown sugar, ketchup, and barbecue sauce into the oven.

7. Add the yellow mustard and the chili powder to the oven. Stir everything well.

8. Once the beans begin to boil, place the lid on the oven and remove about 12 coals from underneath the oven to reduce the heat.

**FINAL PREPARATION STEP FOR ADULTS:**
About 15 minutes after the Scouts put the lid on the oven, refresh the coals with 12 new briquettes, then continue to simmer beans with the lid on for about another hour.

**Tom Reis, Johnston, Iowa**
Committee Member
Troop 44, Mid-Iowa Council

**DANGER ZONE:**

- Hot coals! Enforce your fire-safe zone and use your gloves.
- Sharp utensils! Careful chopping required.
- Raw meat! Sanitize your hands after handling.
- Hot and heavy cookware! Use your gloves.

**HOT TIP!**
For even thicker sauce and deeper flavor, the beans can be simmered for as long as 4 hours provided that the coals are occasionally refreshed.

# Peas and Onions Gone Wild

"This recipe was the only way I could get the kids to eat onions. It's fantastic. Who doesn't like food with a cream sauce?"

## INGREDIENTS

2 pounds frozen peas

1 pound frozen pearl onions

¼ cup all-purpose flour

1 cup half-and-half

½ teaspoon ground thyme

½ teaspoon ground black pepper

1 teaspoon salt

## REQUIRED EQUIPMENT:

Cookstove
Medium-size cook pot
Wooden spoon

## INITIAL PREPARATION STEPS FOR ADULTS:

1. Set frozen peas and onions in a warm location to thaw about an hour before dinner.

2. Prepare cookstove once it's time to cook.

## PREPARATION STEPS FOR YOUNG SCOUTS:

1. Pour the flour into a medium-size cook pot.

2. Add about 2 tablespoons of the half-and-half to the flour and stir it well with a wooden spoon until a thick paste forms with no lumps left in it.

3. Pour the rest of the half-and-half (a little less than 1 cup) into the flour paste, then add the thyme, pepper, and salt and stir it all well.

4. Add the thawed peas and pearl onions to the pot. Stir again until all the vegetables are covered in the cream sauce.

5. Place the pot on the stove and turn the heat to a medium flame, halfway between the lowest and highest settings.

6. Stir frequently while warming the peas and onions for about 10 minutes. If the sauce begins to stick or burn, lower the flame.

7. Turn off the stove.

**Chef's Corner**

If half-and-half were added all at once to the flour, many lumps would form that would then be almost impossible to break up. But by adding a little liquid first to create a paste, the lumps are much easier to eliminate.

**DANGER ZONE:**

• Hot pot! Turn the handle inward and be careful not to spill contents.

**Kathleen Kirby, Milltown, New Jersey**
Merit Badge Counselor
Troop 33, Central New Jersey Council

Servings: 11 to 13
Preparation Time—Total: 30 minutes
Preparation Time—For the Scouts: 30 minutes
Recommended Number of Chefs: 1 Scout and 1 adult
Challenge Level: Easy

The combination of flavors is fantastic! *Christine Conners*

# Great Southwest Skillet Mashed Potatoes

## REQUIRED EQUIPMENT:
Cookstove
Medium-size mixing bowl
Wooden spoon
Chef's knife
Large frying pan

## INITIAL PREPARATION STEPS FOR ADULTS:
1. Prepare cookstove for the Scouts.

2. Be prepared to help the Scouts with frying the bacon.

## PREPARATION STEPS FOR YOUNG SCOUTS:
1. Dump instant mashed potatoes into a medium-size bowl.

2. Pour the milk and the 3½ cups of water into the bowl.

3. Add the dried parsley, garlic salt, and dried onion flakes to the bowl. Stir everything well with a wooden spoon until all large lumps are gone.

4. Slice the bacon into bite-size pieces using a chef's knife.

5. Place a large frying pan on the stove, then set the flame to medium height, about halfway between the lowest and highest settings. Add the bacon to the frying pan.

6. Fry the bacon until it's fully cooked, but not too crispy. Ask an adult to help determine when it's ready.

7. Pour the mashed potato mixture from the bowl into the frying pan with the bacon.

8. Stir the potatoes and bacon together with the wooden spoon until they're well mixed.

9. Cook for a few minutes, stirring occasionally. Turn off the stove once the potatoes are heated through, then serve.

**Vince Wahler, Albuquerque, New Mexico**
Assistant Scoutmaster
Troop 395, Great Southwest Council

## INGREDIENTS
4 cups Hungry Jack instant mashed potatoes

2 cups milk

3½ cups water

1 tablespoon dried parsley

2 teaspoons garlic salt

1 tablespoon dried onion flakes

1 pound bacon

### DANGER ZONE:
- Sharp utensils! Careful slicing required.

- Raw meat! Sanitize your hands after handling.

- Hot and heavy cookware! Keep frying pan handle turned inward.

- Hot grease! Protect your hands and forearms from splattering bacon.

Servings: 14 to 16
Preparation Time—Total: 30 minutes
Preparation Time—For the Scouts: 30 minutes
Recommended Number of Chefs: 2 Scouts and 1 adult
Challenge Level: Moderate

# Popcorn on the Grill

### INGREDIENTS

¼ **cup vegetable oil**

¾ **cup popping corn**

**Optional: ¼ cup melted butter**

**Salt to taste**

**HOT TIP!**
The fire pit doesn't necessarily need to have a grate over it for this recipe to work. But it's difficult to shake a large pan using tongs at just the right height over the fire for minutes on end.

### REQUIRED EQUIPMENT:

Folding camp grill (if fire pit doesn't have a grate)
11 x 9 x 2-inch aluminum pan (or larger)
Heavy-duty aluminum foil
Long-handled tongs

### INITIAL PREPARATION STEPS FOR ADULTS:

1. Prepare a wood fire, allowing it to die down to low embers before cooking.

2. If the fire pit doesn't have a built-in grate, set up a folding camp grill over the embers. The heat needs to be pretty high to pop corn, so make sure the grate isn't too far from the embers.

3. Be ready to help the Scouts in the third step below with placing the foil cover on the pan.

### PREPARATION STEPS FOR YOUNG SCOUTS:

1. Pour the vegetable oil into an aluminum pan. Swirl the oil around so that it covers the entire bottom of the pan.

2. Sprinkle the popping corn into the pan so that the kernels are evenly distributed in the oil.

3. Tear off a sheet of foil that's about a foot longer than the pan. Lay the foil over the pan and seal it by pinching the foil onto the edges of the pan. Make sure that the foil is not tightly stretched over the pan. It should be loosely fitted so that, once the corn pops, it will have room to grow into a "dome" under the foil.

4. Place the pan on the grill grate.

5. Use long-handled tongs to grab the edge of the pan and then continuously shake the pan back and forth. Constantly shaking the pan is a very important step to avoid burning the popcorn.

Servings: 4 to 6
Preparation Time—Total: 1 hour and 15 minutes
(including 1 hour to prepare the fire)
Preparation Time—For the Scouts: 15 minutes
Recommended Number of Chefs: 1 Scout and 1 adult
Challenge Level: Moderate

6. Depending on how hot the embers are, it can take several minutes before the corn starts to pop. So don't give up. Once the corn begins to pop, it will gradually pick up tempo.

7. The corn may pop for several minutes. Once the rate of popping begins to really die down, remove the pan from the grill. If you waited until the last stragglers popped, much of the corn would probably have charred by then.

8. Remove the foil, being careful not to burn yourself on the escaping steam. Pour optional melted butter over the popcorn, then sprinkle on a little salt to taste.

**Tim and Christine Conners, Statesboro, Georgia**
Committee Members and Merit Badge Counselors
Troop 340, Coastal Empire Council

It doesn't take long to make a load of fresh popcorn over a fire. *Christine Conners*

# Scarecrow Corn

**INGREDIENTS PER SERVING**

1 corn on the cob, with husk intact

Butter to taste

Salt to taste

Optional: Old Bay Seasoning to taste

"Have you ever thought about how challenging it is to get fruit and vegetables from the farm to your table? Before the food even reaches the grocery store, it may have to survive drought, flooding, frost, disease, insects, and even birds! The next time you are on a country drive, see if you can't spot a scarecrow, basically a large, funny-looking stuffed doll on a pole often set near a garden. He might look scary, but his job isn't to scare people. It's to scare away the birds who might try to eat the crops!"

**REQUIRED EQUIPMENT:**

Folding camp grill (if fire pit doesn't have a grate)
Large cook pot
Long-handled tongs

**INITIAL PREPARATION STEPS FOR ADULTS:**

1. Prepare a wood fire, allowing it to die down to low embers before cooking.

2. If the fire pit doesn't have a built-in grate, set up a folding camp grill over the embers.

3. Fill a large pot with water for soaking the corn.

**PREPARATION STEPS FOR YOUNG SCOUTS:**

1. Peel back the green husk covering the ear of corn, but don't tear any of the husk leaves off.

2. Pick off all of the stringy corn silks. Rinsing in water can help remove the silks if they are stuck to the ear.

3. Now pull the husk back up to completely cover the kernels.

4. Place the corn in the pot of cold water to soak for about 15 minutes.

5. Use tongs to set the soaked ear of corn on the grill over the fire. Be sure the husks are covering all of the kernels.

Servings: 1—multiply as required
Preparation Time—Total: 1 hour and 30 minutes (including 1 hour to prepare the fire)
Preparation Time—For the Scouts: 30 minutes
Recommended Number of Chefs: 1 Scout and 1 adult
Challenge Level: Easy

6. Cook for about 10 minutes. Occasionally rotate the ear of corn. Keep a close watch on the husk to be sure it doesn't catch fire.

7. Remove the corn from the grill, peel off the husk, then cover the kernels with butter and sprinkle with salt to taste. If you'd like, sprinkle on a little optional Old Bay Seasoning at this time.

**Mille Hutchison, Pittsburgh, Pennsylvania**
Trainer
Girl Scouts of Western Pennsylvania

**DANGER ZONE:**

- Live fire! Use barbecue gloves while working with a wood fire.

**HOT TIP!**
Soaking the corn in water helps to keep the husk from burning while it's cooking. This step makes the recipe so easy. No wrapping in foil is required!

## Veggie Herd

"This recipe is absolutely delicious, even for Scouts who don't usually like green beans."

**INGREDIENTS**
Cooking spray

2 (15-ounce) cans sliced new potatoes

2 (14.5-ounce) cans sliced green beans

1 teaspoon Lawry's Seasoned Salt

1 cup shredded cheddar Jack cheese

### REQUIRED EQUIPMENT:
Folding camp grill (if fire pit doesn't have a grate)
Heavy-duty aluminum foil, 18 inches wide
Can opener
Long-handled tongs

### INITIAL PREPARATION STEPS FOR ADULTS:
1. Prepare a wood fire, allowing it to die down to low embers before cooking.

2. If the fire pit doesn't have a built-in grate, set up a folding camp grill over the embers.

### PREPARATION STEPS FOR YOUNG SCOUTS:
1. Tear off a sheet of foil about 3 feet long and place it on a clean, flat surface. Be sure the foil is the wide type. Spray the foil with cooking spray.

2. Open the cans of sliced potatoes and green beans, then drain the liquid from all of the cans. You won't be using the liquid.

3. Spread the sliced potatoes closer to one end of the foil. Do it like this, instead of putting them in the center of the foil, because you'll be folding the other half of the foil over the top of the vegetables to seal them.

4. Pour the sliced green beans over the potatoes.

5. Sprinkle the Lawry's Seasoned Salt over the green beans and potatoes.

6. Cover the vegetables with the shredded cheddar Jack cheese.

Servings: 10 to 12
Preparation Time—Total: 1 hour and 30 minutes (including 1 hour to prepare the fire)
Preparation Time—For the Scouts: 30 minutes
Recommended Number of Chefs: 1 Scout and 1 adult
Challenge Level: Moderate

7. Bring the half of the foil with no vegetables on it over the top of the veggie stack, then fold each of the three open edges over on itself several times for a tight seal. If you have trouble understanding this step, ask an adult for help.

8. Carefully lay the packet on the grill over the embers using barbecue gloves and tongs. You'll need two hands to do this. If you have trouble, ask an adult for help!

9. Heat for 7 to 8 minutes, then flip the packet using tongs and heat for another 7 to 8 minutes.

**FINAL PREPARATION STEP FOR ADULTS:**
Help the Scouts remove the foil packet from the fire and be sure to give the packet a few minutes to cool before opening.

**Kathleen Kirby, Milltown, New Jersey**
Merit Badge Counselor
Troop 33, Central New Jersey Council

### DANGER ZONE:

• Live fire! Use barbecue gloves while working with a wood fire.

• Hot steam! Use care to avoid burns when opening the foil packet.

# Ambrosia Salad

"The word 'ambrosia' comes from Greek mythology and literally means 'food of the gods.' It's not surprising, then, that variations of this recipe are called ambrosia, because they're heavenly!"

## INGREDIENTS

2 (20-ounce) cans crushed pineapple

2 (15-ounce) cans mandarin oranges

2 cups mini marshmallows

2 cups sweetened coconut flakes

1 (8-ounce) container whipped topping

## REQUIRED EQUIPMENT:

Can opener
Large mixing bowl
Wooden spoon

## PREPARATION STEPS FOR YOUNG SCOUTS:

1. Pour the cans of crushed pineapple into a large bowl.

2. Drain the cans of mandarin oranges, then pour the orange segments into the bowl with the pineapple.

3. Add the mini marshmallows and coconut flakes to the bowl.

4. Scoop the whipped topping into the bowl.

5. Mix all the ingredients well with a wooden spoon, then serve.

**Donna Pettigrew, Anderson, Indiana**
Tanglewood Camp Director and Master Trainer
Girl Scouts of Central Indiana

Servings: 14 to 16
Preparation Time—Total: 15 minutes
Preparation Time—For the Scouts: 15 minutes
Recommended Number of Chefs: 1 Scout and 1 adult
Challenge Level: Easy

# Funky Fruit Salad

## REQUIRED EQUIPMENT:
Chef's knife
Medium-size bowl
Wooden spoon

## INITIAL PREPARATION STEPS FOR ADULTS:
1. Keep the fruit chilled in the cooler until it's time to prepare the fruit salad.

2. Demonstrate to the Scouts how to cut a peach around the pit so they can tackle the job next time.

## PREPARATION STEPS FOR YOUNG SCOUTS:
1. Slice the seedless grapes in half using a chef's knife, then put the grape pieces into a medium-size bowl.

2. Peel an orange, pull the wedges apart, then cut each wedge into four pieces. Place the pieces of orange in the bowl.

3. Peel a banana, cut it into thin slices, and put these into the bowl.

4. The peach or nectarine should have had the pit removed already. If not, ask an adult for help. Once the pit is removed, chop the peach or nectarine into bite-size cubes. Place the pieces in the bowl.

5. Pour the blueberries into the bowl, then gently stir all the fruit together with a wooden spoon.

6. If the fruit salad won't be served immediately, cover the bowl with a lid or sheet of foil, then place the bowl in a cooler until mealtime.

**Donna Pettigrew, Anderson, Indiana**
Tanglewood Camp Director and Master Trainer
Girl Scouts of Central Indiana

## INGREDIENTS
2 cups seedless grapes
1 orange
1 banana
1 peach or nectarine
1 pint fresh blueberries

### DANGER ZONE:
• Sharp utensils! Careful chopping required.

### HOT TIP!
For a creamy fruit salad, mix ½ cup blended peach yogurt into the fruit salad.

Servings: 8 to 10
Preparation Time—Total: 30 minutes
Preparation Time—For the Scouts: 30 minutes
Recommended Number of Chefs: 2 Scouts and 1 adult
Challenge Level: Moderate

# Backcountry Biscuits

## INGREDIENTS

¼ cup (½ standard stick) butter

Vegetable oil for greasing Dutch oven

2 cups unbleached self-rising flour, plus a little more for dusting hands

½ teaspoon salt

1 tablespoon granulated sugar

1 cup whole milk

## REQUIRED EQUIPMENT:

12-inch camp Dutch oven
Briquettes and accessories for Dutch oven
Large mixing bowl
Wooden spoon

## INITIAL PREPARATION STEPS FOR ADULTS:

1. Set the butter in a warm location to soften about an hour before starting coals.

2. Grease Dutch oven with a little vegetable oil.

3. Prepare 33 briquettes.

## PREPARATION STEPS FOR YOUNG SCOUTS:

1. Pour 2 cups of the flour into a large mixing bowl. Do this while an adult prepares the Dutch oven.

2. Add the salt and sugar to the bowl. Mix using a wooden spoon.

3. Pour the milk into the bowl, then add the half-stick of softened butter.

4. Mix the flour and other ingredients in the bowl using clean hands. Squish the dough again and again until no large lumps remain.

5. Grab bits of dough and roll them in the palms of your hands into balls about 2 inches in diameter (a little larger than a golf ball). If the dough sticks to your hands in large lumps, rub some flour on your hands and fingers to help keep it from doing that.

6. Set each dough ball inside the Dutch oven, side by side with the others. You should have about 6 to 8 biscuits when finished.

Servings: 6 to 8
Preparation Time—Total: 45 minutes
Preparation Time—For the Scouts: 45 minutes
Recommended Number of Chefs: 2 Scouts and 1 adult
Challenge Level: Moderate

7. Place the lid on the Dutch oven. Once the adult says the coals are ready, place 22 coals on the lid and 11 coals underneath the oven. Make sure the coals aren't clumped together.

8. Bake for 20 to 30 minutes, until the dough balls have turned into biscuits and the tops of the biscuits have become lightly browned. Ask an adult to help if you're not sure if the biscuits are ready to serve.

## FINAL PREPARATION STEP FOR ADULTS:
If need be, assist the Scouts with determining when the biscuits are ready to serve.

**Tim and Christine Conners, Statesboro, Georgia**
Committee Members and Merit Badge Counselors
Troop 340, Coastal Empire Council

### DANGER ZONE:
• Hot coals! Enforce your fire-safe zone and use your gloves.

• Hot and heavy cookware! Use your gloves.

### HOT TIP!
This recipe purposely puts the decision making on the young Scouts to determine when the biscuits are ready to eat. Adults, be prepared to help them with the judgment call.

# Drumbeat Strawberry Bread

"We've all heard that bread is the 'stuff of life,' but that doesn't mean you have to eat the boring, store-bought, white kind on a campout. Why not try this unique recipe with your fellow campers? With a little supervision, Scouts will not only gain confidence in their cooking skills but have fun making their own unique, sweet-tasting version."

## INGREDIENTS

1 (20-ounce) package frozen strawberries

4 eggs

¾ cup vegetable oil

1 cup chopped walnuts or pecans

3 cups all-purpose flour

1¾ cups granulated sugar

1 teaspoon baking soda

1 teaspoon salt

Cooking spray

## REQUIRED EQUIPMENT:

12-inch camp Dutch oven
Briquettes and accessories for Dutch oven
2 large mixing bowls
Chef's knife
Wooden spoon
Heavy-duty aluminum foil

## INITIAL PREPARATION STEPS FOR ADULTS:

1. About an hour before starting the coals, set the frozen strawberries out to thaw if they haven't already.

2. Prepare 25 briquettes for the Dutch oven.

## PREPARATION STEPS FOR YOUNG SCOUTS:

1. Crack the eggs into a large bowl, then mix them by stirring very quickly with a fork. Do this while an adult prepares the coals.

2. Chop the strawberries into small pieces with a chef's knife. Place these in the bowl with the eggs.

3. Pour the vegetable oil and chopped nuts into the bowl with the eggs and strawberries. Mix everything well with a wooden spoon.

4. In another large bowl, pour the flour, sugar, baking soda, and salt. Mix these together with the wooden spoon.

5. Stir the egg and strawberry mixture one more time, then pour it into the bowl with the flour mixture. Stir all the ingredients together with the spoon until it forms a thick batter.

**HOT TIP!**
Don't substitute fresh strawberries for the thawed frozen strawberries. The extra liquid that comes from the thawed strawberries is essential for this recipe.

Servings: 14 to 16
Preparation Time—Total: 1 hour and 30 minutes
Preparation Time—For the Scouts: 30 minutes
Recommended Number of Chefs: 2 Scouts and 1 adult
Challenge Level: Moderate

6. Cover the inside of the Dutch oven with aluminum foil. Press it tightly against the bottom and wall, then spray the foil with cooking spray.

7. Pour the batter into the Dutch oven. It's helpful to have two people working this step, one to hold the bowl, the other to scoop the batter into the oven.

8. Once the adult says the coals are ready, put the lid on the oven, then set the oven on a metal tray. Place 8 coals under the oven and 17 on the lid.

**FINAL PREPARATION STEP FOR ADULTS:**
Bake for 1 hour or until a knife or toothpick inserted into the bread comes out clean. Depending on how long it takes the Scouts to prepare the batter, a refreshing of the coals may be required.

**Carl Laub, Arlington Heights, Illinois**
Executive Board Member
Northwest Suburban Council

**DANGER ZONE:**
- Hot coals! Enforce your fire-safe zone and use your gloves.
- Raw eggs! Sanitize your hands after handling.
- Sharp utensils! Careful chopping required.
- Hot and heavy cookware! Use your gloves.

Strawberry Bread tastes as good as it looks! *Christine Conners*

# Indian Corn Cakes

**INGREDIENTS**

1 (8.5-ounce) package Jiffy corn muffin mix

1 egg

⅓ cup milk

2 tablespoons butter

**REQUIRED EQUIPMENT:**

Cookstove
Quart-size ziplock freezer bag
Medium-size frying pan
Spatula

**INITIAL PREPARATION STEP FOR ADULTS:**

Prepare cookstove for the Scouts.

**PREPARATION STEPS FOR YOUNG SCOUTS:**

1. Pour the corn muffin mix into a quart-size ziplock bag.

2. Ask someone to hold the bag while you crack the egg into it and then add the milk.

3. Seal the bag tightly while squeezing the air out, then carefully squish the ingredients together in the bag until all the large lumps are gone.

4. Place a medium-size frying pan on the stove, then turn the flame to a medium-low height, closer to the lowest setting than to the highest.

5. Melt the butter in the warm frying pan, then spread the melted butter around using a spatula.

6. Pinch a bottom corner of the ziplock bag to move the muffin batter out of it, then cut the corner off using a pair of scissors. The corner cut should be about ½ inch long.

7. Squirt some of the batter out of the bag's corner cut into the hot frying pan like you might do for pancakes. Form as many corn cakes as will fit in the pan, but keep them at least an inch apart from each other at first, because the batter will expand.

8. Once the corn cakes begin to bubble slightly, flip them with the spatula, then cook for a minute or two before removing them from the pan.

9. Continue cooking the same way until the batter is used up.

10. Turn off the stove once finished.

**DANGER ZONE:**

• Hot and heavy cookware! Keep frying pan handle turned inward.

Servings: 4 to 6
Preparation Time—Total: 30 minutes
Preparation Time—For the Scouts: 30 minutes
Recommended Number of Chefs: 1 Scout and 1 adult
Challenge Level: Moderate

**Tim and Christine Conners, Statesboro, Georgia**
Committee Members and Merit Badge Counselors
Coastal Empire Council

# Muffin in an Orange

"The orange skins provide natural bowls for the baked muffins while infusing the muffins with a wonderful citrusy flavor."

## REQUIRED EQUIPMENT:
Chef's knife
Medium-size mixing bowl
Wooden spoon
Heavy-duty aluminum foil
Long-handled tongs

## INITIAL PREPARATION STEP FOR ADULTS:
Prepare a wood fire, allowing it to die down to low embers before cooking.

## PREPARATION STEPS FOR YOUNG SCOUTS:

1. Cut each of the oranges in half using a chef's knife.

2. Scoop out the insides of the oranges, being careful not to tear the skins. The insides aren't required for this recipe, so pass around the pieces of orange to the Scouts to eat. You'll end up with eight hollowed-out orange halves, like little bowls.

3. Pour the blueberry muffin mix into a medium-size bowl.

4. Crack the egg into the bowl, then add the milk. Stir the ingredients with a wooden spoon until the batter is thick and no large lumps remain.

5. Fill each of the orange halves with muffin batter. Any batter left over can be added to more hollowed-out orange halves, if you have them.

6. Tear off four large squares of heavy-duty foil.

## INGREDIENTS
4 medium-size oranges

1 (7-ounce) package Jiffy blueberry muffin mix

1 egg

⅓ cup milk

**HOT TIP!**
The mechanics of this recipe are easy. What makes it more difficult is the challenge of knowing when the muffin batter is fully cooked.

Servings: 4
Preparation Time—Total: 1 hour and 30 minutes (including 1 hour to prepare the fire)
Preparation Time—For the Scouts: 30 minutes
Recommended Number of Chefs: 2 Scouts and 1 adult
Challenge Level: Moderate

7. Align two filled orange halves together to form a sphere, working quickly to keep the batter from oozing out. Wrap the sphere tightly in a sheet of foil. Do this for all of the orange halves. You should have four foil-wrapped orange spheres once finished.

8. Set the foil spheres directly onto the hot coals using long-handled tongs.

9. Bake the oranges for about 10 to 15 minutes, at which point the muffin mix should be fully cooked.

**Donna Pettigrew, Anderson, Indiana**
Tanglewood Camp Director and Master Trainer
Girl Scouts of Central Indiana

These Webelos are demonstrating one variation for this recipe: They're using half an orange to form the bowl, then leaving the top of the foil packet open while baking. *Beverly Jo Antonini*

# Snake on a Stick

"Camping in Pennsylvania, our Tenderfoot Scouts started cooking Snakes on a Stick for their patrol. Then the older patrols couldn't resist. They all loved it! A word of advice: bring extra cans of the biscuits, because no one can eat just one!"

**INGREDIENTS**

1 (16.3-ounce) container Pillsbury Original Home-style Grands! refrigerated biscuits

1 (8-ounce) can Kraft Sharp Cheddar Easy Cheese

Cooking spray

## REQUIRED EQUIPMENT:

1 cooking stick per Scout, each with a stem about the width of a dime and about 3 feet long, all side branches removed

## INITIAL PREPARATION STEPS FOR ADULTS:

1. Prepare a wood fire. It's tough to cook anything over a roaring fire without burning it, so allow the fire time to die down to low embers before cooking.

2. Assist the Scouts in finding suitable cooking sticks. Never cut green limbs from live trees and shrubs. Use sticks already on the ground. And never gather sticks from around poisonous trees and shrubs, such as oleander or poison sumac!

## PREPARATION STEPS FOR YOUNG SCOUTS:

1. Open the container of biscuit dough and separate the biscuits from each other. There will be a total of eight.

2. Shape each biscuit dough into a "snake" about 1 foot long. Roll out any lumpy parts of the dough so that the snake is evenly thick.

3. Completely cover about 1 foot along the end of each stick with cooking spray, then wrap the dough around the part of the stick covered in oil. Twist the dough around the stick like the stripes on a candy cane, starting at the top end of the stick and working downward. It's okay if the dough touches as you go.

**HOT TIP!**
You can substitute honey, jelly, or peanut butter for the cheese.

Servings: 8

Preparation Time—Total: 1 hour and 30 minutes (including 1 hour to prepare the fire)

Preparation Time—For the Scouts: 30 minutes

Recommended Number of Chefs: 1 Scout per serving and 1 adult

Challenge Level: Moderate

4. Hold the dough-wrapped stick over the hot embers and rotate the stick often to cook all sides of the dough.

5. Heat the dough until it becomes golden brown all over, then remove the stick from over the fire. Patiently hold the stick for a few minutes while the bread cools off.

6. Once the bread cools, carefully wiggle it off the end of the stick.

7. Eat the biscuit bread plain or fill the hole with cheese from the squirt can.

**Kathleen Kirby, Milltown, New Jersey**
Merit Badge Counselor
Troop 33, Central New Jersey Council

No one can resist warm bread fresh from the fire! *Christine Conners*

# Superhero Sweet Biscuits

"Every superhero has a sweet side!"

**REQUIRED EQUIPMENT:**
12-inch camp Dutch oven
Briquettes and accessories for Dutch oven
Small bowl
Heavy-duty aluminum foil

**INITIAL PREPARATION STEP FOR ADULTS:**
Prepare 25 briquettes for the Dutch oven.

**PREPARATION STEPS FOR YOUNG SCOUTS:**

1. Mix the cinnamon and brown sugar in a small bowl with a spoon. Do this while an adult prepares the coals for the Dutch oven.

2. Cover the inside of the Dutch oven with aluminum foil. Press it tightly against the bottom and wall.

3. Open the container of biscuit dough by whomping it on the side of something hard, like a picnic table. Remove the dough and pull it apart into eight dough disks.

4. Lay the biscuit dough disks side by side in the Dutch oven.

5. Pour the cream over the biscuits, coating all of them.

6. Sprinkle all of the biscuits with the cinnamon-sugar mixture from the small bowl.

7. Once the adult says the coals are ready, put the lid on the oven, then set the oven on a metal tray. Place 8 coals under the oven and 17 on the lid.

8. Bake the biscuits for about 30 minutes. Allow to cool for a few minutes before serving.

**Beverly Jo Antonini, Morgantown, West Virginia**
Assistant Scoutmaster
Troop 49, Mountaineer Area Council

**INGREDIENTS**
2 teaspoons ground cinnamon

1 cup brown sugar

1 (16.3-ounce) container Pillsbury Original Home-style Grands! refrigerated biscuits

1 cup heavy cream

**DANGER ZONE:**

- Hot coals! Enforce your fire-safe zone and use your gloves.

- Hot and heavy cookware! Use your gloves.

Servings: 8
Preparation Time—Total: 45 minutes
Preparation Time—For the Scouts: 45 minutes
Recommended Number of Chefs: 1 Scout and 1 adult
Challenge Level: Easy

# S'mores Dip

**INGREDIENTS**

1 (11.5-ounce) package milk chocolate chips

2 cups mini marshmallows

1 (14.4-ounce) package graham crackers

**REQUIRED EQUIPMENT:**

12-inch camp Dutch oven with trivet
Briquettes and accessories for Dutch oven
9-inch pie pan

**INITIAL PREPARATION STEP FOR ADULTS:**

Prepare 21 briquettes for the Dutch oven.

**PREPARATION STEPS FOR YOUNG SCOUTS:**

1. Pour chocolate chips into a pie pan, then spread them around so they are distributed evenly. Do this while an adult prepares the coals.

2. Spread the mini marshmallows over the chocolate chips. Make sure the marshmallows are evenly distributed.

3. Set the pie pan on a trivet in the Dutch oven.

4. Once the adult says the coals are ready, put the lid on the oven, then set the oven on a metal tray. Place 6 coals under the oven and 15 coals on the lid.

**FINAL PREPARATION STEPS FOR ADULTS:**

1. Bake for 40 minutes until the chocolate chips and marshmallows turn soft and just begin to melt. Don't overcook the dip or use too much heat, or the chocolate can become gritty.

2. Set the pie pan on the serving table. While the dip is still soft, scoop it up with the graham crackers.

**Tim and Christine Conners, Statesboro, Georgia**
Committee Members and Merit Badge Counselors
Troop 340, Coastal Empire Council

---

**Chef's Corner**
Everyone has heard of s'mores, but do you know what the name means? It's a contraction of "some more," as in "I'd like some more"!

---

**DANGER ZONE:**

• Hot coals! Enforce your fire-safe zone and use your gloves.

• Hot and heavy cookware! Use your gloves.

---

Servings: 6 to 8
Preparation Time—Total: 1 hour
Preparation Time—For the Scouts: 15 minutes
Recommended Number of Chefs: 1 Scout and 1 adult
Challenge Level: Easy

# Johnny Appleseed's Baked Apples

"Johnny Appleseed, whose real name was John Chapman, was an American pioneer in the early 1800s. He is best known for planting many thousands of apple trees over a span of about fifty years. His dream was to plant so many apple trees that no one would ever go hungry. Two hundred years later, some of those trees still bear fruit!"

**INGREDIENTS**
7 small Granny Smith apples
½ cup raisins
½ cup brown sugar
1 teaspoon ground cinnamon
¼ cup (½ standard stick) butter

**REQUIRED EQUIPMENT:**
12-inch camp Dutch oven with trivet
Briquettes and accessories for Dutch oven
Paring knife
Narrow metal spoon
Small bowl
9-inch pie pan
Long-handled tongs

**INITIAL PREPARATION STEPS FOR ADULTS:**

1. Prepare 23 briquettes for the Dutch oven.

2. Assist the Scouts with coring the apples. This step is a little tricky, because the bottom of each apple needs to remain intact. Make an initial circular cut with a paring knife at the top of the apple, then dig the core out using a narrow spoon. Remember not to puncture the bottom of the apple.

**HOT TIP!**
The baked apples go great with a little whipped cream or kick-the-can ice cream.

**PREPARATION STEPS FOR YOUNG SCOUTS:**

1. Pour the raisins, brown sugar, and cinnamon into a bowl. Mix the ingredients together with a spoon.

2. Fill the hole in each of the apples with the raisin mixture.

3. Cut the half-stick of butter into seven slices and push a slice into the top of the hole in each of the apples.

4. Place a pie pan on a trivet inside the Dutch oven. Don't know what a trivet is? Ask an adult to show you.

Servings: 7
Preparation Time—Total: 1 hour
Preparation Time—For the Scouts: 1 hour
Recommended Number of Chefs: 3 Scouts and 1 adult
Challenge Level: Moderate

5. Set the apples side by side, hole facing upward, in the pie pan in the Dutch oven.

6. Once the adult says the coals are ready, put the lid on the oven, then set the oven on a metal tray. Place 7 coals under the oven and 16 on the lid.

7. Bake for about 30 minutes.

8. Carefully remove the apples from the hot oven using tongs. Set the apples in a safe location to cool for about 10 minutes before serving.

**Beverly Jo Antonini, Morgantown, West Virginia**
Assistant Scoutmaster
Troop 49, Mountaineer Area Council

Like an apple pie turned inside out! *Christine Conners*

# Monkey Bread

**REQUIRED EQUIPMENT:**
12-inch camp Dutch oven
Briquettes and accessories for Dutch oven
Heavy-duty aluminum foil
Small bowl
Wooden spoon
Small cook pot

**INGREDIENTS**
½ cup (1 standard stick) butter

Cooking spray

1 cup granulated sugar

1 tablespoon ground cinnamon

2 (16-ounce) containers refrigerated biscuit dough

**INITIAL PREPARATION STEPS FOR ADULTS:**
1. Set the butter in a warm location to soften about an hour before starting coals.

2. Prepare 25 briquettes for the Dutch oven.

**PREPARATION STEPS FOR YOUNG SCOUTS:**
1. Cover the inside of the Dutch oven with aluminum foil. Press it tightly against the bottom and wall, then spray the foil with cooking spray. Do this while an adult prepares the coals.

2. Pour the sugar and cinnamon into a small bowl and mix them together with a wooden spoon.

3. Break open the cans of dough and separate the biscuits from each other.

4. Tear each of the biscuits into four pieces. Gently roll each piece into a ball with clean hands. Try not to mash the dough down while you're doing it.

5. Roll each biscuit ball in the sugar-cinnamon mixture.

6. Place the coated dough balls in the Dutch oven side by side. If they need to be stacked, add them to the center of the oven first, then fill outward toward the edge.

7. Once the adult says the coals are ready, drop the softened stick of butter into a small cook pot, then hold the pot over the coals while the butter melts. Use barbecue gloves to protect your hands from the heat.

Servings: 8 to 10
Preparation Time—Total: 1 hour
Preparation Time—For the Scouts: 1 hour
Recommended Number of Chefs: 2 Scouts and 1 adult
Challenge Level: Moderate

8. Pour any remaining sugar and cinnamon from the bowl into the pot with the melted butter and stir it all together with the wooden spoon.

9. Pour the sugar-butter mixture over the dough balls in the oven. Be sure to coat all of them.

10. Put the lid on the oven, then set the oven on a metal tray. Place 8 coals under the oven and 17 on the lid.

11. Bake the monkey bread for 20 to 25 minutes until it becomes golden brown.

12. Remove the lid from the oven and allow the monkey bread to cool for a few minutes. The lumps of bread can then be broken apart using the wooden spoon before carefully serving.

**Michael Trdy, Cameron, Texas**
Scoutmaster
Troop 752, Longhorn Council

## Chef's Corner

According to Wikipedia, monkey bread is also called monkey puzzle bread, sticky bread, golden crown, pinch-me cake, pluck-it cake, bubbleloaf, and monkey brains!

## DANGER ZONE:

• Hot coals! Enforce your fire-safe zone and use your gloves.

• Hot and heavy cookware! Use your gloves.

# Charlie Brown's Great Pumpkin Delight

"If the Great Pumpkin doesn't show up on Halloween night, here's the next best thing!"

## REQUIRED EQUIPMENT:
12-inch camp Dutch oven
Briquettes and accessories for Dutch oven
2 medium-size mixing bowls
Can opener
Wooden spoon
Heavy-duty aluminum foil

## INITIAL PREPARATION STEPS FOR ADULTS:
1. About an hour before starting the coals, set the butter sticks in a warm location to soften.

2. Prepare 25 briquettes for the Dutch oven.

## PREPARATION STEPS FOR YOUNG SCOUTS:
1. Crack the eggs into a medium-size bowl, then mix them by stirring very quickly with a fork. Do this while an adult prepares the coals for the Dutch oven.

2. Scrape the contents of the large can of pumpkin pie mix into the bowl with the eggs, then add the can of evaporated milk. Mix everything well with a wooden spoon.

3. Cover the inside of the Dutch oven with aluminum foil. Press the foil tightly against the bottom and wall. Spray the foil with cooking spray.

4. Pour the pumpkin mixture into the Dutch oven.

5. Dump the yellow cake mix into a medium-size bowl. Use a clean bowl, not the same one used to prepare the pumpkin mixture.

## INGREDIENTS
1 cup (2 standard sticks) butter

3 eggs

1 (30-ounce) can pumpkin pie mix

1 (5-ounce) can evaporated milk

Cooking spray

1 (18.5-ounce) package yellow cake mix

**HOT TIP!**
It's easy to confuse canned pumpkin pie mix with canned pure pumpkin. Don't use canned pure pumpkin in this recipe!

Servings: 13 to 15
Preparation Time—Total: 1 hour and 15 minutes
Preparation Time—For the Scouts: 15 minutes
Recommended Number of Chefs: 2 Scouts and 1 adult
Challenge Level: Easy

6. Drop the softened sticks of butter into the yellow cake mix and stir them together. After most of the butter is coated by the cake mix, use clean hands to squish the mix together with your fingertips until it is crumbly.

7. Sprinkle the cake mix crumbles over the pumpkin mix in the oven.

8. Once the adult says the coals are ready, put the lid on the oven, then set the oven on a metal tray. Place 8 coals under the oven and 17 on the lid.

**FINAL PREPARATION STEP FOR ADULTS:**
Bake for about 60 minutes. Refresh the coals if required.

**Beverly Jo Antonini, Morgantown, West Virginia**
Assistant Scoutmaster
Troop 49, Mountaineer Area Council

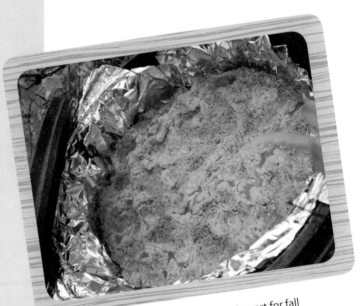

Great Pumpkin Delight is the perfect dessert for fall camping. *Christine Conners*

# Chocolaty Lava Cake

"My son has gluten intolerance, so there are very few desserts he can eat. I came up with Chocolaty Lava Cake to make his camping trips tastier. This recipe is delicious and pleases all the Scouts."

## REQUIRED EQUIPMENT:
12-inch camp Dutch oven
Briquettes and accessories for Dutch oven
Heavy-duty aluminum foil
Wooden spoon
Large mixing bowl

## INITIAL PREPARATION STEPS FOR ADULTS:
1. About an hour before starting the coals, set the butter in a warm place to soften.

2. Prepare 25 briquettes for the Dutch oven.

3. About 45 minutes after starting the first batch of coals, begin a second batch of 25.

## PREPARATION STEPS FOR YOUNG SCOUTS:
1. Cover the inside of the Dutch oven with aluminum foil. Press it tightly against the bottom and wall, then spray the foil with cooking spray. Do this while an adult prepares the coals.

2. Open the containers of chocolate frosting and, using a wooden spoon or spatula, spread the frosting over the aluminum foil on the bottom of the oven.

3. Pour the packages of cake mix into a large bowl.

4. Crack the eggs over the cake mix in the bowl, then drop in the sticks of softened butter.

5. Add the 2 cups of water to the bowl. Mix everything very well with a wooden spoon until no large lumps remain.

## INGREDIENTS
1 cup (2 standard sticks) butter

Cooking spray

2 (16-ounce) containers chocolate fudge frosting

2 (15-ounce) packages Betty Crocker gluten free devil's food cake mix

6 eggs

2 cups water

Servings: 18 to 20
Preparation Time—Total: 1 hour and 45 minutes
Preparation Time—For the Scouts: 30 minutes
Recommended Number of Chefs: 2 Scouts and 1 adult
Challenge Level: Moderate

6. Pour the cake batter into the oven. Do not stir!

7. Once the adult says the coals are ready, put the lid on the oven, then set the oven on a metal tray. Place 8 coals under the oven and 17 on the lid.

## FINAL PREPARATION STEPS FOR ADULTS:

1. Bake for about 60 to 70 minutes, refreshing the coals as needed.

2. Remove from the coals, take the lid off, and allow the cake to cool for about 15 minutes before serving.

**Sarah Myers, Irmo, South Carolina**
Scout Mom
Troop 413, Indian Waters Council

**HOT TIP!** The frosting gets very hot after baking and can burn one's mouth. So be sure to allow the cake to cool after removing from the coals and before serving.

# Apple Gingerbread Dumplings

## REQUIRED EQUIPMENT:
Cookstove
Medium-size mixing bowl
Wooden spoon
Medium-size cook pot with lid

## INITIAL PREPARATION STEP FOR ADULTS:
Prepare cookstove.

## PREPARATION STEPS FOR YOUNG SCOUTS:
1. Dump the gingerbread cake mix into a medium-size bowl, then add the ⅓ cup of water to the bowl. Stir with a wooden spoon until the water is all absorbed. The batter will be very thick.

2. Pour the applesauce into a cook pot, then place the pot over a low flame on the stove.

3. Warm the applesauce for about 10 minutes. Stir it often to prevent popping bubbles.

4. Use the spoon to carefully drop blobs of the gingerbread cake mix onto the hot applesauce in the pot. Don't stir the gingerbread! It's supposed to sit on top of the applesauce.

5. Set the lid on the pot and continue to cook for about 10 minutes over a very low flame.

6. Turn off the stove.

7. Remove the pot from the stove and allow the gingerbread to cool for a few minutes before serving with whipped topping.

**Kathleen Kirby, Milltown, New Jersey**
Merit Badge Counselor
Troop 33, Central New Jersey Council

## INGREDIENTS
1 (15.25-ounce) package Betty Crocker gingerbread cake and cookie mix

⅓ cup water

1 (48-ounce) jar cinnamon-flavored applesauce

1 (8-ounce) container whipped topping

**Chef's Corner**
In this recipe, the rising steam from the applesauce bakes the gingerbread. No need for an oven!

**DANGER ZONE:**
- Hot pot! Turn the handle inward and be careful not to spill contents.

Servings: 13 to 15
Preparation Time—Total: 30 minutes
Preparation Time—For the Scouts: 30 minutes
Recommended Number of Chefs: 1 Scout and 1 adult
Challenge Level: Easy

# Chocolate Bark

**INGREDIENTS**

1 cup milk chocolate chips

1 cup salted roasted peanuts

**REQUIRED EQUIPMENT:**

Cookstove
Medium-size cook pot
Wooden spoon
Wax paper
Cooler filled with ice

**INITIAL PREPARATION STEP FOR ADULTS:**

Prepare cookstove.

**PREPARATION STEPS FOR YOUNG SCOUTS:**

1. Pour the chocolate chips into a medium-size cook pot, then place the pot on the stove over a low flame.

2. Stir the chocolate chips constantly using a wooden spoon until all the chips are completely melted.

3. Turn the flame off, then remove the pot from the stove.

4. Add the peanuts to the melted chocolate. Stir with the wooden spoon until all the peanuts are coated.

5. Tear off a sheet of wax paper about 2 feet long.

6. Use the wooden spoon to scoop spoonfuls of chocolate and peanuts onto the wax paper. Don't allow the chocolate-peanut blobs to touch each other.

**FINAL PREPARATION STEPS FOR ADULTS:**

1. Let the chocolate cool down for about 15 minutes.

2. Carefully move the sheet of "bark" to a cooler filled with ice. Set the wax paper on a plate or tray, if necessary, to keep it from becoming waterlogged.

3. Shut the cooler and allow the bark to chill for about 30 minutes, until the chocolate is firm.

**Donna Pettigrew, Anderson, Indiana**
Tanglewood Camp Director and Master Trainer
Girl Scouts of Central Indiana

**DANGER ZONE:**

• Hot pot! Turn the handle inward and be careful not to spill contents.

**HOT TIP!**
To avoid cross-contamination of the bark, don't chill it in a cooler that contains raw meat or eggs.

Servings: 6 to 8
Preparation Time—Total: 1 hour
Preparation Time—For the Scouts: 15 minutes
Recommended Number of Chefs: 2 Scouts and 1 adult
Challenge Level: Easy

# Paul Bunyan Apple Pie

"Paul Bunyan, the giant lumberjack of folklore, was so big at birth that it took five storks to deliver him. He ate so much as a child that his mother had to feed him ten barrels of porridge every morning so his stomach wouldn't rumble and shake their house to the ground. His camp stove was an acre in size, and his griddle so large that it had be greased by men using huge slices of bacon as skates!"

## REQUIRED EQUIPMENT:

Folding camp grill (if fire pit doesn't have a grate)
Heavy-duty aluminum foil
Can opener
Large spoon
Long-handled tongs

## INITIAL PREPARATION STEPS FOR ADULTS:

1. Set butter in a warm location to soften about an hour before starting coals.

2. Prepare a wood fire, allowing it to die down to low embers before cooking.

3. If the fire pit doesn't have a built-in grate, set up a folding camp grill over the embers.

## PREPARATION STEPS FOR YOUNG SCOUTS:

1. Tear off four sheets of aluminum foil, each about 1 foot long.

2. Lay out the bread, then spread the half-stick of soft butter over only one side of each slice.

3. Set a slice of bread closer to the edge of one side on each of the four foil pieces, with the buttered side facing the foil.

4. Spread a can of apple pie filling over the slices of bread on the foil sheets. Use a large spoon for this. Divide the filling evenly among the four slices.

## INGREDIENTS

¼ cup (½ standard stick) butter

8 slices white bread

1 (21-ounce) can apple pie filling

1 tablespoon ground cinnamon

2 tablespoons granulated sugar

Servings: 8
Preparation Time—Total: 1 hour and 30 minutes (including 1 hour to prepare the fire)
Preparation Time—For the Scouts: 30 minutes
Recommended Number of Chefs: 2 Scouts and 1 adult
Challenge Level: Moderate

5. Sprinkle the cinnamon evenly over the pie filling on the four slices. Do the same with the sugar.

6. Lay a slice of buttered bread on top of the pie filling on each of the four pieces of foil, making sure that the buttered side is facing upward, not toward the apples.

7. Bring the empty half of each foil sheet over the top of its bread stack, then fold each of the three open edges on each foil sheet over on itself several times for a tight seal. If you have trouble understanding this step, ask an adult for help.

8. Lay each packet on the grill over the embers using tongs.

9. Heat for 3 to 5 minutes, then flip the packets and heat for another 3 to 5 minutes.

10. Remove the packets from the fire and allow them to cool for a few minutes.

**FINAL PREPARATION STEPS FOR ADULTS:**

1. Help the Scouts open their packets, making sure they first give their food a few minutes to cool off.

2. Divide each pie into 2 servings.

**Scott Simerly, Apex, North Carolina**
Senior Assistant Scoutmaster
Troop 204, Occoneechee Council

**HOT TIP!**
Try cherry or blueberry pie filling too. Time and again, however, the favorite of many Scouts is apple pie filling with cinnamon and sugar.

# Berry Bread Pudding

**REQUIRED EQUIPMENT:**
Folding camp grill (if fire pit doesn't have a grate)
Medium-size mixing bowl
Wooden spoon
Heavy-duty aluminum foil, 18-inch wide roll
Long-handled tongs

**INITIAL PREPARATION STEPS FOR ADULTS:**
1. Prepare a wood fire, allowing it to die down to low embers before cooking.

2. Set frozen berries in a warm location to soften about an hour before cooking.

3. Move the fire pit's grill grate into position over the fire. If the fire pit doesn't have a built-in grate, set up a folding camp grill over the embers.

**PREPARATION STEPS FOR YOUNG SCOUTS:**
1. Crack the eggs into a medium-size bowl, then add the milk, sugar, and cinnamon. Stir everything well with a wooden spoon.

2. Dump the bread cubes into the bowl. The bread cubes can be made by gently tearing or cutting slices of bread into bite-size pieces. You'll need about half of a regular loaf of bread for this.

3. Add the thawed berries to the bowl. Stir all the ingredients well once again.

4. Tear off a long sheet of foil, about 2 feet long, then spray it with cooking spray.

5. Dump the berry-pudding mixture on one end of the sheet of foil but don't let it spill over the edges.

**INGREDIENTS**

**1 cup frozen berries, your choice**

**2 eggs**

**1 cup milk**

**½ cup granulated sugar**

**¼ teaspoon ground cinnamon**

**4 cups bread cubes (about half a loaf)**

**Cooking spray**

Servings: 5 to 7
Preparation Time—Total: 1 hour and 45 minutes (including 1 hour to prepare the fire)
Preparation Time—For the Scouts: 45 minutes
Recommended Number of Chefs: 2 Scouts and 1 adult
Challenge Level: Easy

6. Bring the half of the foil with no food on it over the top of the berry pudding, then fold each of the three open edges over on itself several times for a tight seal. If you have trouble understanding this step, ask an adult for help.

7. Lay the foil packet on the grill grate over the embers.

8. Heat the packet for about 10 minutes, then flip and heat for another 10 minutes.

9. Remove the packet from the fire using long-handled tongs.

### FINAL PREPARATION STEP FOR ADULTS:
Carefully open the foil packet for the Scouts, being careful of the escaping steam.

**Allison Rudick, Trussville, Alabama**
Leader
Troop 872, Girl Scouts of North-Central Alabama

# Dirty Marshmallows

"Take your roasted marshmallows to a whole new level!"

## REQUIRED EQUIPMENT:
Folding camp grill (if fire pit doesn't have a grate)
Serving plate
Small cook pot
Wooden spoon
Camping forks, one for each of the Scouts

## INGREDIENTS
1 (7-ounce) package sweetened coconut flakes

1 (12-ounce) package semisweet chocolate chips

1 (10-ounce) package regular marshmallows

## INITIAL PREPARATION STEPS FOR ADULTS:
1. Prepare a wood fire. Allow the fire time to die down to low embers before cooking.

2. Move the fire pit's grill grate into position over the fire. If the fire pit does not have a built-in grate, set up a folding grill over the embers.

## PREPARATION STEPS FOR YOUNG SCOUTS:
1. Spread the coconut flakes on a serving plate.

2. Pour the chocolate chips into a small cook pot, then set the pot on the grill over the embers.

3. Stir the chips with a wooden spoon after a few minutes. The chocolate chips may look like they aren't melting, but don't be fooled. They'll be soft.

4. Continue to stir frequently until the chips completely melt, then move the pot to a safe location on a table. Don't allow the chocolate to become too hot.

5. Pass around camping forks and marshmallows and have the Scouts roast their own marshmallows over the embers.

Servings: 5 to 7
Preparation Time—Total: 1 hour and 15 minutes (including 1 hour to prepare the fire)
Preparation Time—For the Scouts: 15 minutes
Recommended Number of Chefs: 1 Scout per serving and 1 adult
Challenge Level: Moderate

6. Direct each Scout to dip their marshmallows in the melted chocolate, then roll the chocolate-covered marshmallows in the coconut flakes. This will be easier to do, and more sanitary, if the Scouts keep their marshmallows on the camping forks while dipping and rolling.

**Donna Pettigrew, Anderson, Indiana**
Tanglewood Camp Director and Master Trainer
Girl Scouts of Central Indiana

**HOT TIP!**
Try substituting chopped nuts or candy sprinkles for the coconut flakes, or sliced bananas for the marshmallows.

Say goodbye to plain ol' roasted marshmallows!
Christine Conners

# Scout Taffy

"Young Scouts love making this taffy! They become entranced by the way the consistency of the marshmallow morphs into something totally different."

## REQUIRED EQUIPMENT:
None

## INITIAL PREPARATION STEP FOR ADULTS:
Be sure all the Scouts thoroughly wash their hands before beginning this recipe. Have plenty of water available for cleaning up afterward.

## PREPARATION STEPS FOR YOUNG SCOUTS:
1. With clean hands, hold a marshmallow between your thumb and forefinger.

2. Using your thumb and forefinger on the other hand, pinch the marshmallow and pull to stretch it (but don't break it).

3. Now fold the pulled piece of marshmallow back to the other hand, pinch it, and stretch it again.

4. Keep folding and pulling until the marshmallow turns into taffy.

**Kathleen Kirby, Milltown, New Jersey**
Merit Badge Counselor
Troop 33, Central New Jersey Council

## INGREDIENTS
1 (8-ounce) package regular-size strawberry flavored marshmallows

**DANGER ZONE:**
- Germs! All diners must have clean hands.

**HOT TIP!**
Try other flavors of marshmallows with this recipe.

Servings: 4 to 8
Preparation Time—Total: 5 minutes
Preparation Time—For the Scouts: 5 minutes
Recommended Number of Chefs: 1 Scout per serving and 1 adult
Challenge Level: Easy

# Edible Campfire

"This is a fun way to demonstrate to young Scouts how to make a basic campfire."

## INGREDIENTS PER SERVING

1 medium-size flour tortilla

1 tablespoon peanut butter

About 30 mini marshmallows or mini jelly beans

1 large pretzel stick

3 small pretzel sticks

1 teaspoon sweetened coconut flakes

5 Red Hots candies or candy corn

1 small paper cup filled with chocolate milk or fruit juice

**HOT TIP!**
More "logs" can be used to form a "teepee" or "log cabin" to demonstrate other fire-building techniques.

**REQUIRED EQUIPMENT PER SERVING:**
Regular paper plate
Small paper cup

**PREPARATION STEPS FOR EACH SCOUT:**

1. Lay your tortilla flat on your paper plate.

2. Spread a tablespoon of peanut butter into a circle about the size of a baseball at the center of the tortilla. This will help to keep the other pieces in place.

3. Surround the peanut butter with a circle of mini marshmallows or jelly beans. These are the "campfire stones" to make your "fire ring."

4. Break a large pretzel stick into three pieces then lay the pieces on top of each other to form a triangle in the middle of the fire ring. These are the "logs."

5. Break small pretzel sticks in half and pile the pieces inside the log triangle to form the "kindling." Top the kindling with coconut flakes, the "tinder."

6. Lay the Red Hots candies or candy corn among the kindling to form the "fire."

7. Serve with a small paper cup filled with chocolate milk or fruit juice. This is the "fire bucket"!

**Donna Pettigrew, Anderson, Indiana**
Tanglewood Camp Director and Master Trainer
Girl Scouts of Central Indiana

Servings: 1—multiply as required
Preparation Time—Total: 15 minutes
Preparation Time—For the Scouts: 15 minutes
Recommended Number of Chefs: 1 Scout per serving and 1 adult
Challenge Level: Easy

With this recipe, young Scouts can 1) learn proper fire building techniques, 2) play with their food, then 3) eat it!
Christine Conners

# Moose Lips

**REQUIRED EQUIPMENT:**
Chef's knife
Paring knife

**INITIAL PREPARATION STEP FOR ADULTS:**
Slicing apples can be a challenge, especially when the cores are tough. Assist the Scouts as needed with this preparation step and be sure that all wedges have the seeds removed.

**PREPARATION STEPS FOR YOUNG SCOUTS:**
1. Use a chef's knife to cut a large apple in half from top to bottom, then slice each of these pieces in half from top to bottom. You'll have four pieces at this point.

2. Now cut each of the pieces in half once more, top to bottom, for a total of eight apple wedges.

3. Use a small paring knife to remove the core and seeds from each piece of apple.

4. Smear a small amount of peanut butter on the inside (white) part of each wedge.

5. Set 4 or 5 marshmallows into the peanut butter on each of four wedges. The peanut butter helps the marshmallows to stay in place.

6. Set another wedge with peanut butter on top of the marshmallows on the first wedge to form a pair of "lips." Do this for the remaining wedges, and you'll have four sets. Do you see the moose lips smiling back at you?

**Ken Harbison, Rochester, New York**
Former Boy Scout
Washington Trails Council

**INGREDIENTS**
1 large red apple

16 to 20 mini marshmallows

1 rounded tablespoon peanut butter

**DANGER ZONE:**
• Sharp utensils! Careful slicing required.

Who wouldn't love lips like these? *Christine Conners*

Servings: 4
Preparation Time—Total: 15 minutes
Preparation Time—For the Scouts: 15 minutes
Recommended Number of Chefs: 2 Scouts and 1 adult
Challenge Level: Moderate

# Powwow Pudding Cones

## INGREDIENTS

1 (5.7-ounce) package instant pudding, your choice of flavor

1 (2.6-ounce) package Dream Whip whipped topping mix

2 cups cold milk

6 ice cream cones or cups

Pudding Cones are the next best thing to soft-serve ice cream! *Christine Conners*

## REQUIRED EQUIPMENT:
Quart-size ziplock freezer bag

## PREPARATION STEPS FOR YOUNG SCOUTS:

1. Pour the pudding mix into a quart-size ziplock bag.

2. Open the box of Dream Whip. There will be two packets inside. Pour the contents of both packets into the bag containing the pudding mix.

3. Pour the cold milk into the ziplock bag.

4. Seal the ziplock bag, then check again to be sure it's tightly closed.

5. Hold the bag with both hands at the top, keeping the seal shut with your fingers, then shake it for a few seconds.

6. Keep holding the bag at the top with one hand while squeezing it with the other hand. Continue to knead the mix until it's free of lumps and the pudding becomes firm. This will take about 5 minutes.

7. Pinch a bottom corner of the ziplock bag to move the pudding mix out of it, then cut the corner off using a pair of scissors or a small knife. The corner cut should be about ½ inch long.

8. Carefully squeeze the pudding mix through the cut corner of the bottom of the bag into each of six ice cream cones or cups. Try to put an equal amount into all the cones. Ask someone to help hold the cones if you have trouble doing it yourself.

**Kathleen Kirby, Milltown, New Jersey**
Merit Badge Counselor
Troop 33, Central New Jersey Council

Servings: 6
Preparation Time—Total: 15 minutes
Preparation Time—For the Scouts: 15 minutes
Recommended Number of Chefs: 1 Scout and 1 adult
Challenge Level: Easy

**HOT TIP!**
The milk needs to be cold for the pudding to thicken properly. If the mix is slow to become firm while kneading, place the sealed bag on ice in a clean cooler for a few minutes.

# GORP Buffet

"This recipe allows Scouts to personalize their own trail mix, particularly good for large groups or picky eaters."

## REQUIRED EQUIPMENT:
Quart-size ziplock freezer bags, 1 for each person
5 medium-size bowls
5 large spoons or measuring cups

## INITIAL PREPARATION STEPS FOR ADULTS:
1. You'll have five types of ingredients for this recipe: cereal, nuts, dried fruit, snacks, and candy. Pour each of the five ingredients into its own bowl.

2. Set a large serving spoon or measuring cup in each bowl. These will be used for scooping ingredients.

3. Instruct the Scouts to fill their quart-size bags between one-quarter and half full. This serving size should last them much of the day for snacking in camp or on the trail.

4. Watch to be sure the Scouts don't overindulge in any particular ingredient, especially the snacks and candy, as they fill their bags. To avoid a shark-feed, it may be best to have no more than a couple of Scouts at a time in the "buffet line."

## PREPARATION STEP FOR EACH SCOUT:
Scoop your favorite ingredients into the ziplock bag using the cup or spoon, not your hands. Go easy on the snacks and candy. If you don't like one type of ingredient, double up on another healthier choice.

**Kathleen Kirby, Milltown, New Jersey**
Merit Badge Counselor
Troop 33, Central New Jersey Council

## INGREDIENTS
(select 1 item from each category; choose 12- to 16-ounce packages for each)

**Cereal:**
Chex, Cheerios, Cocoa Puffs, Froot Loops, Life, Teddy Grahams

**Shelled Nuts:**
Almonds, cashews, peanuts, pecans, walnuts, mixed nuts

**Dried Fruit:**
Apples, apricots, bananas, cherries, pears, raisins, Craisins, strawberries

**Snacks:**
Bugles, Cheez-Its, mini pretzels, oyster crackers, veggie chips

**Candy:**
Candy corn, Hot Tamales, M&Ms, mini marshmallows, Skittles

### DANGER ZONE:
- Germs! All diners must have clean hands.

### Chef's Corner
Ever wonder what "gorp" means? It's actually an acronym, G.O.R.P., which stands for "good ol' raisins and peanuts." Of course, nowadays, GORP mixes contain almost anything, and many don't even contain raisins and peanuts!

Servings: About 15
Preparation Time—Total: 15 minutes
Preparation Time—For the Scouts: 5 minutes
Recommended Number of Chefs: 1 Scout per serving and 1 adult
Challenge Level: Easy

## INGREDIENTS

1 (8.9-ounce) package regular Cheerios

1 (12-ounce) package raisins

1 (19.2-ounce) package plain M&Ms

1 (34.5-ounce) container dry roasted peanuts

1 (10-ounce) package mini marshmallows

**HOT TIP!**
Trail mixes make great outdoor snacks because they are tasty and don't need refrigeration. It's also easy to make endless varieties by substituting your favorite ingredients.

# Tanglewood Trail Mix

"A tasty, fuel-loaded trail mix that is sure to bring smiles to any hike. Stretch your legs and walk while enjoying this snack."

## REQUIRED EQUIPMENT:

Large mixing bowl
Wooden spoon
26 sandwich-size ziplock bags

## PREPARATION STEPS FOR YOUNG SCOUTS:

1. Dump all the ingredients into a very large bowl: the Cheerios, raisins, M&Ms, dry roasted peanuts, and mini marshmallows.

2. Gently mix all the ingredients together with a wooden spoon. Don't crush the Cheerios.

3. Scoop 1 cup of trail mix into a sandwich-size ziplock bag, then seal the bag tightly. Repeat this process until all the trail mix is used up. You should be able to fill about 26 bags with the mix.

4. Hand a bag of trail mix to each of the campers in your group. Snack on the mix throughout the day around camp or while hiking.

**Donna Pettigrew, Anderson, Indiana**
Tanglewood Camp Director and Master Trainer
Girl Scouts of Central Indiana

Colorful and tasty with lots of healthy bits thrown in . . . the perfect snack for a day hike.
*Christine Conners*

Servings: About 26
Preparation Time—Total: 15 minutes
Preparation Time—For the Scouts: 15 minutes
Recommended Number of Chefs: 2 Scouts and 1 adult
Challenge Level: Easy

156

# Abominable Snowman Ice Cream

"This recipe is named for the mysterious apelike creature that legend says roams the cold and high Himalayan Mountains."

### REQUIRED EQUIPMENT:
Quart-size ziplock freezer bag
Gallon-size ziplock freezer bag
Duct tape
Heavy gloves or towel

### PREPARATION STEPS FOR YOUNG SCOUTS:

1. While one Scout holds a quart-size ziplock freezer bag open, pour in the half-and-half, sugar, vanilla extract, and flavored syrup.

2. Carefully close the ziplock bag while squeezing as much air out of it as you can. Be certain that it's sealed tightly. Fold the seal over and tape it down along its length with duct tape. This is insurance to be certain salt water doesn't get inside.

3. Place the filled quart-size bag in a gallon-size ziplock freezer bag.

4. Add the crushed ice to the gallon-size bag along with the rock salt and the half-cup of water.

5. Now seal the large bag the same way as the smaller bag, squeezing out the air, sealing it tightly, then using duct tape to be sure it won't leak.

6. Wearing heavy gloves or using a towel to protect your hands from the cold, begin to gently massage the bag. The half-and-half mixture will slowly turn into ice cream. This can take 15 to 30 minutes, so patience is required. Keep kneading the bag, passing it off to another to help as your hands become tired.

### INGREDIENTS
2 cups half-and-half

¼ cup granulated sugar

1 teaspoon vanilla extract

¼ cup chocolate, strawberry, or butterscotch syrup

5 cups ice

¾ cup rock salt

½ cup water

Servings: 4 to 6
Preparation Time—Total: 30 minutes
Preparation Time—For the Scouts: 30 minutes
Recommended Number of Chefs: 2 Scouts and 1 adult
Challenge Level: Easy

7. The ice cream is ready once it becomes like soft-serve. (It will never turn hard, so don't expect that.) Tear or cut open the gallon bag to drain the salt water. Do this over gravel or in a sink, not over grass or vegetation, because the salt can kill it.

8. Open the quart bag containing the ice cream, then scoop it out to serve. The corner of the bag can also be cut open and the ice cream squeezed into individual cups.

**Georgia Bosse, Portland, Oregon**
Leave-No-Trace Master Educator
Girl Scouts of Oregon and Southwest Washington

**DANGER ZONE:**

- Intense cold! Use gloves or a towel to protect your fingers.

HOT TIP!
Try topping your ice cream with chocolate chips, blueberries, or chopped frozen strawberries.

# American Flag Cake

"A great treat anytime, but especially during the summertime national holidays!"

**REQUIRED EQUIPMENT:**
Chef's knife
13 x 9-inch aluminum cake pan
Wooden spoon
Spatula

**PREPARATION STEPS FOR YOUNG SCOUTS:**

1. Cut the pound cake into ten slices of equal thickness using a chef's knife.

2. Trim the hulls (leafy green tops) from the strawberries.

3. Slice each strawberry in half from top to bottom, then slice each piece of strawberry in two once again, top to bottom. You'll have four pieces from each strawberry.

4. Lay the slices of pound cake side by side in the aluminum cake pan.

5. With a wooden spoon, cover the pound cake slices with all of the whipped topping, then use the spoon to smooth it out so it is evenly thick.

6. Now design an American flag using the berries. First, arrange a rectangle full of blueberries by setting them in the whipped topping in a corner of the cake. Next, make several red stripes using the slices of strawberries.

7. Be sure to show off the cake with great fanfare before serving with a spatula.

**Tim and Christine Conners, Statesboro, Georgia**
Committee Members and Merit Badge Counselors
Troop 340, Coastal Empire Council

**INGREDIENTS**
1 (16-ounce) package Sara Lee All Butter pound cake

1 pound fresh strawberries

1 (16-ounce) container whipped topping

1 pint fresh blueberries

**DANGER ZONE:**
- Sharp utensils! Careful slicing required.

Awesome and easy to make, this refreshing, patriotic treat is perfect anytime during the warm summer months. *Christine Conners*

Servings: 10
Preparation Time—Total: 30 minutes
Preparation Time—For the Scouts: 30 minutes
Recommended Number of Chefs: 2 Scouts and 1 adult
Challenge Level: Easy

# Fire Cider

**INGREDIENTS PER SERVING**
1 cup apple cider

1 tablespoon Red Hots candies

**REQUIRED EQUIPMENT:**
Cookstove
Medium-size cook pot
Wooden spoon
1 mug per serving

**INITIAL PREPARATION STEP FOR ADULTS:**
Prepare cookstove.

**PREPARATION STEPS FOR YOUNG SCOUTS:**

1. For each serving, pour 1 cup of apple cider into a cook pot.

2. Set the flame to a medium-low height, closer to the lowest setting than the highest.

3. Add 1 tablespoon of Red Hots candies to the cider.

4. Warm the cider until it is steaming but not boiling.

5. Turn off the stove.

6. Stir the cider with a wooden spoon for several seconds.

7. Pour the cider into a mug and serve.

**Tony Neubauer, Piscataway, New Jersey**
Committee Chairperson
Troop 67, Central New Jersey Council

**DANGER ZONE:**

• Hot pot! Turn the handle inward and be careful not to spill contents.

Servings: 1— multiply as required
Preparation Time—Total: 15 minutes
Preparation Time—For the Scouts: 15 minutes
Recommended Number of Chefs: 1 Scout and 1 adult
Challenge Level: Easy

# Jell-O Juice

**REQUIRED EQUIPMENT:**
Cookstove
Small cook pot
2 mugs

**INITIAL PREPARATION STEP FOR ADULTS:**
Prepare cookstove.

**PREPARATION STEPS FOR YOUNG SCOUTS:**
1. Pour the 2 cups of water into a small cook pot.

2. Set the flame on the highest setting, then bring the water to a boil.

3. Turn off the stove.

4. Carefully pour the hot water into two mugs, dividing the water evenly between them.

5. Divide the Jell-O powder between the mugs. This can be done by carefully opening the Jell-O packet, then measuring out the contents with a spoon, adding a spoonful to one mug, then a spoonful to the second, and repeating until the Jell-O is used up.

6. Stir the Jell-O into the hot water with the spoon, then serve.

**Tim and Christine Conners, Statesboro, Georgia**
Committee Members and Merit Badge Counselors
Troop 340, Coastal Empire Council

**INGREDIENTS**
**2 cups water**

**1 (3-ounce) package Jell-O gelatin, your choice of flavor**

**DANGER ZONE:**
• Hot pot! Turn the handle inward and be careful not to spill contents.

Servings: 2— multiply as required
Preparation Time—Total: 15 minutes
Preparation Time—For the Scouts: 15 minutes
Recommended Number of Chefs: 1 Scout and 1 adult
Challenge Level: Easy

# Caveman's Cocoa

*"Pound your chest! Stomp your feet! Caveman's Cocoa can't be beat!"*

## INGREDIENTS

2 (12-ounce) cans evaporated milk

2 cups chocolate syrup

4 cups water

Optional: mini marshmallows

### REQUIRED EQUIPMENT:

Cookstove
Can opener
Medium-size cook pot
Wooden spoon
1 mug per serving

### INITIAL PREPARATION STEP FOR ADULTS:

Prepare cookstove.

### PREPARATION STEPS FOR YOUNG SCOUTS:

1. Pour the evaporated milk into a medium-size cook pot.

2. Add the chocolate syrup and water to the pot. Stir well with a wooden spoon.

3. Set the flame to a medium-low height, closer to the lowest setting than the highest.

4. Warm the milk until it is steaming but not boiling.

5. Turn off the stove.

6. Pour the cocoa into mugs and serve, topped with optional marshmallows.

**Donna Pettigrew, Anderson, Indiana**
Tanglewood Camp Director and Master Trainer
Girl Scouts of Central Indiana

## DANGER ZONE:

• Hot pot! Turn the handle inward and be careful not to spill contents.

Servings: 10
Preparation Time—Total: 15 minutes
Preparation Time—For the Scouts: 15 minutes
Recommended Number of Chefs: 1 Scout and 1 adult
Challenge Level: Moderate

# Orangutan Orange Drink

"Tastes like a Creamsicle!"

**REQUIRED EQUIPMENT:**
Medium-size mixing bowl
Wooden spoon

**PREPARATION STEPS FOR YOUNG SCOUTS:**

1. Pour the Tang drink mix into a medium-size bowl.

2. Dump the contents of the package of vanilla pudding into the bowl with the Tang.

3. Stir the pudding mix and Tang together with a wooden spoon.

4. For each serving, pour about 1 cup of milk into a drinking glass, then add about 2 tablespoons of the drink mix. Stir well with a spoon.

**Tim and Christine Conners, Statesboro, Georgia**
Committee Members and Merit Badge Counselors
Troop 340, Coastal Empire Council

**INGREDIENTS**
½ cup orange-flavored Tang drink mix

1 (5.1-ounce) package vanilla Jell-O instant pudding and pie filling

10 cups (2½ quarts) milk

**HOT TIP!**
If the dry drink mix isn't all used at the same time, pour what's left into a ziplock bag to save for later.

Servings: 10
Preparation Time—Total: 5 minutes
Preparation Time—For the Scouts: 5 minutes
Recommended Number of Chefs: 1 Scout and 1 adult
Challenge Level: Easy

# Lazy Lemonade

**INGREDIENTS**
6 large lemons

1 cup granulated sugar

7 cups  water

**REQUIRED EQUIPMENT:**
Chef's knife
2-quart container
Wooden spoon

**PREPARATION STEPS FOR YOUNG SCOUTS:**

1. Slice 6 large lemons in half crosswise using a chef's knife.

2. With clean hands, squeeze each of the lemon halves into a container that can hold at least 2 quarts of water. Try to get as much juice from each lemon as you can. Using two hands to squeeze can help do this.

3. Pour the sugar into the container.

4. Add the water to the container and stir well with a wooden spoon.

**Maria Conners, Statesboro, Georgia**
Former Girl Scout
Girl Scouts of Historic Georgia

**DANGER ZONE:**
• Sharp utensils! Careful slicing required.

Servings: 8
Preparation Time—Total: 15 minutes
Preparation Time—For the Scouts: 15 minutes
Recommended Number of Chefs: 1 Scout and 1 adult
Challenge Level: Easy

# Appendix A

# SIMPLE MEASUREMENT CONVERSIONS

## United States Conversions

1 dash . . . . . . . . . . . . . . . ⅛ teaspoon

1 tablespoon . . . . . . . . . . . 3 teaspoons

1 ounce . . . . . . . . . . . . . . 2 tablespoons

¼ cup . . . . . . . . . . . . . . . 2 ounces (4 tablespoons)

⅓ cup . . . . . . . . . . . . . . . 5 tablespoons + 1 teaspoon

½ cup . . . . . . . . . . . . . . . 4 ounces (8 tablespoons)

1 cup . . . . . . . . . . . . . . . 8 ounces

1 pint . . . . . . . . . . . . . . . 2 cups  (16 ounces)

1 quart . . . . . . . . . . . . . . 2 pints, or 4 cups (32 ounces)

1 gallon . . . . . . . . . . . . . . 4 quarts, or 16 cups (128 ounces)

# International Metric Conversions

## Volume and Weight

| United States | Metric |
|---|---|
| 1 teaspoon | 5 milliliters |
| 1 tablespoon | 15 milliliters |
| 1 ounce (volume) | 30 milliliters |
| ¼ cup | 60 milliliters |
| ½ cup | 120 milliliters |
| ¾ cup | 180 milliliters |
| 1 cup | 240 milliliters |
| 1 pint | 0.48 liters |
| 1 quart | 0.95 liters |
| 1 gallon | 3.79 liters |
| 1 ounce (weight) | 28 grams |
| 1 pound | 0.45 kilograms |

## Temperature

| Degrees F | Degrees C |
|---|---|
| 175 | 80 |
| 200 | 95 |
| 225 | 105 |
| 250 | 120 |
| 275 | 135 |
| 300 | 150 |
| 325 | 165 |
| 350 | 175 |
| 375 | 190 |
| 400 | 205 |
| 425 | 220 |
| 450 | 230 |
| 475 | 245 |
| 500 | 260 |

# Appendix B

# LOW-IMPACT COOKING

"Leave a place better than you found it." A Scout hears that phrase innumerable times over the years. In fact, low-impact wilderness ethics has become a core principle within Scouting, the mastery of which is a requirement for rank advancement.

Early Scoutcraft emphasized skills for adapting the camp environment to suit the needs of the outdoorsman. But in more recent years, with increasing use of and pressure on our wild places, the emphasis has rightly shifted toward developing wilderness skills within the context of minimizing one's impact on the outdoors and others.

In fact, the Outdoor Code of the Boy Scouts of America states:

> *As an American, I will do my best to*
> *Be clean in my outdoor manners*
> *Be careful with fire*
> *Be considerate in the outdoors*
> *Be conservation-minded*

By conscientiously following the Scout Outdoor Code, we become better and more thoughtful stewards of our natural resources.

The Leave No Trace Center for Outdoor Ethics also provides a set of principles that are becoming increasingly well known and applied within Scouting. These align closely with the Scout Outdoor Code. The principles of outdoor ethics from Leave No Trace enhance those of the Scout Outdoor Code by providing additional detail on their application.

The seven core principles of Leave No Trace are:

1.  Plan ahead and prepare.

2.  Travel and camp on durable surfaces.

3.  Dispose of waste properly.

4.  Leave what you find.

5.  Minimize wood fire impacts.

6.  Respect wildlife.

7.  Be considerate of other visitors.

Careful planning, especially with respect to food preparation, is critical to successfully following the principles of both the Scout Outdoor Code and Leave No Trace, all of which are touched on once at camp. When preparing for an upcoming outing, consider the following list of application points as you discuss food and cooking options with your fellow Scouts and Scouters.

**Choose low-impact methods for preparing your food.**
Some methods of cooking, such as gas stoves and grills, create less impact than others, such as open fires. Low-impact principles are followed when using a camp Dutch oven with charcoal on a fire pan or sheet of foil, provided that the pan or foil is placed on bare soil or rock, and the coal ash is disposed of in a discreet and fire-safe manner.

When using open fire to cook, follow local fire restrictions and use an established fire ring instead of creating a new one. Keep fires small. Collect wood from the ground rather than from standing trees. To avoid creating barren earth, find wood farther away from camp. Select smaller pieces of wood, and burn them completely to ash. Afterward, be sure the fire is completely out, then scatter the ashes. Learn how to use a fire pan or mound fire to prevent scorching the ground and blackening rocks. Don't bring firewood from home to camp if the wood might harbor insects or disease harmful to the flora in your camp area.

**Carefully select and repackage your food to minimize trash.**

Tiny pieces of trash easily become litter. Avoid bringing small, individually packaged candies and other such food items. Twist ties and bread clips are easily lost when dropped. Remove the wrappers and repackage such foods into ziplock bags before leaving home; or use knots, instead of ties and clips, to seal bread bags and the like.

A sheet of foil under this Girl Scout's Dutch oven protects the ground from mess and scarring. There will be no obvious sign that cooking occurred in this location once the Scout is finished. *Allison Rudick*

Metal containers and their lids, crushed beverage cans, and broken glass can easily cut or puncture trash sacks. Wrap them carefully before placing them in thin-wall trash bags. Minimize the use of glass in camp. Scan the camp carefully when packing up to ensure that no litter is left behind.

When cooking for larger groups, it can be even more challenging to maintain a clean camp because of the additional trash that's generated. Have adequate garbage receptacles available at camp and enforce their proper use.

**Minimize leftovers and dispose of food waste properly.**

Leftover foods make for messier trash and cleanup. If poured on open ground, they are unsightly and unsanitary. If buried, animals will dig them up. Leftovers, if not properly managed, encourage problem animals to come into camp. Carefully plan your meals to reduce leftovers. And if any remain, share with others or repackage and set aside in a protected place to eat at a later meal.

Dispose of used wash and rinse water (also called gray water) in a manner appropriate for your camping area. Before disposal, remove or strain food chunks from the gray water and place these with the trash. If no dedicated gray water disposal area is available, scatter the water outside camp in an area free of sensitive vegetation and at least 200 feet from streams and lakes. Avoid excessive sudsing by using only the amount of detergent necessary for the job. Bring only biodegradable detergent and soap to camp.

**Protect your food, trash, and other odorous items from animals.**
Consider avoiding the use of very aromatic foods that can attract animals. Store food, trash, and other odorous items where animals won't be able to get to them. Besides being potentially dangerous to the animal, and inconvenient for the camper, trash is often spread over a large area once the animal gains access. Follow local regulations regarding proper food storage.

**Avoid collecting wild foods.**
Don't harvest wild foods, such as berries, if these are not plentiful in the area you're visiting. Such foods are likely to be a more important component of the local ecosystem when scarce.

These are only a few of the practical considerations and potential applications of the principles of the Scout Outdoor Code and Leave No Trace. Visit www.LNT.org for additional information and ideas.

# Appendix C

# HOW TO MAKE AND USE A SIMPLE BOX OVEN

The box oven is a remarkably simple and reliable outdoor appliance that's easy to build and use. For these reasons, it's been a popular cooking device for many decades within both Boy Scouts of America and Girl Scouts of the USA. While the Dutch oven is the traditional baking appliance of choice for cooking outdoors, its round shape is limiting when baking large rectangular items such as sheet cakes. This is where the box oven excels. And while Dutch ovens aren't unreasonably expensive, you can't beat the price of a box oven, especially considering that it's constructed mostly from scrap!

The construction and use directions for a simple design are provided below and are based on directions and figures provided by Allison Rudick of Troop 872, Girl Scouts of North-Central Alabama.

**Required Materials**
17 x 11-inch (inside dimensions) empty cardboard box, like the kind used for holding ten reams of copy paper
Heavy-duty aluminum foil, 18-inch-wide roll
Duct tape
4 small, flat rocks or similar fireproof objects
4 empty, clean 15-ounce cans, labels removed, all of the exact same size
13 x 9-inch cookie tray
1 small brick or similar-size rock

**Building the Box**

1. Discard the box's lid if it has one. It won't be needed.

2. Tear off a long sheet of foil and push it down into the box so that the sheet runs the long length of the box. Press the foil tight into the corners with the edges of the foil coming up the side walls on the inside of the box. The sheet should be long enough to come up and over the walls at both ends of the box.

3. Run a second long sheet of foil across the narrow width of the box, pressing it into the corners and up and over the walls. The sides of the sheet of foil should overlap the first foil sheet, with all foil now pressed against the walls. Be certain that no cardboard is exposed!

4. For the foil hanging over the walls on the outside of the box, fold it over on itself, then tape it down to the outside of the box using duct tape. The outside of the box does not need to be completely covered in foil. Don't use tape inside the box!

**Using the Oven**

1. Tear off a sheet of wide foil longer than the length of the box. Lay this sheet of foil on level ground, free of debris, in your fire-safe zone. Set a small, flat rock or similar fireproof weight on each of the four corners of the foil.

2. Stand the four empty cans in a rectangular pattern in the center of the foil with the open tops of the cans facing downward. The cans should be arranged with the long length of the rectangle formed by the cans aligned with the long length of the foil. Space the cans so that they will securely support the small cookie tray.

3. Place the cookie tray on the tops of the empty cans. If the tray is unstable, rearrange the cans to improve stability. Be sure the tray is level.

4. Now set the foil-covered box upside down over the top of the cookie tray. Reposition the four rocks previously placed on the foil so that

they are resting under each of the four corners of the box. The rocks are there to hold the box slightly off the ground to allow oxygen to reach the burning coals.

5. With all components in position and ready to go, remove the box until it's time to cook.

6. Prepare standard-size coals as you normally would. When baking, plan to use one briquette for about every 40 degrees Fahrenheit of temperature needed. For example, when baking a pan of brownies at 350°F, you'll need nine briquettes. Note that the maximum practical internal temperature that can be expected with this oven design is about 350–375°F, and baking times longer than about 30 minutes are generally impractical because all the internal heat would be lost if the box were to be lifted to replace the coals.

7. Spread the coals evenly on the sheet of foil on the ground. Distribute them within the perimeter formed by the empty cans. Don't place them where they will be too close to the edges of the box once it's in place!

8. Set the item you're baking, such as a pan of brownie batter, on the cookie sheet. Now place the box over the item you're baking. Be sure that the rocks are under the corners of the box to provide proper ventilation.

The tray support cans and box corner support rocks are positioned, and the coals are being set in place. *Allison Rudick*

9. Place a small brick or similar-size rock on top of the box to give it stability if the day is windy.

10. Time the cooking according to the recipe instructions. The box will become very hot! When removing the box, do so only while wearing protective gloves or using hot pads.

With coals under the baking tray and the box in position, cooking commences. *Allison Rudick*

## Additional Safety Tips

• Before baking food in your box oven for the first time, take it on a test drive. In a fire-safe area, use ten briquettes under the cookie sheet, distributed as if you were actually baking food. Set the box over the coals with proper ventilation and allow the coals to expire on their own, about an hour or so. Remove the box and carefully examine it, inside and out, for any sign of burn damage or weakening, which would likely be due to a lack of foil or a gap between the foil sheets. Correct any deficiencies before using the oven in the field.

• Don't use more than ten coals to help ensure that the temperature inside the box always stays below the ignition point for paper. Never allow coals to come into direct contact with the box.

• Ensure that your oven is operated only in a fire-safe area, and keep it away from low-hanging branches, fuel, or other combustibles. Imagine the box on fire and establish your fire-safe zone accordingly. Have plenty of water on hand to douse flames should it become necessary.

# INDEX

# INDEX

# ABOUT THE AUTHORS

Experienced campers, backpackers, and outdoor chefs, Tim and Christine Conners are the authors of *The Scout's Outdoor Cookbook*, *The Scout's Dutch Oven Cookbook*, *The Scout's Large Groups Cookbook*, and *The Scout's Backpacking Cookbook*, each a collection of unique and outstanding camp recipes from Scout leaders across the United States. Tim and Christine have also penned *Lipsmackin' Backpackin'*, one of the most popular trail cookbooks of the past decade, and *Lipsmackin' Car Campin'*, the latest entry to the Lipsmackin' series of outdoor cookbooks.

Tim and Christine have been testing outdoor recipes for nearly twenty years and have served several times as judges for *Scouting* magazine's prestigious national camp food cooking contest. The Connerses continue to volunteer in various capacities within Boy Scouts of America. They reside with their four children, James, Michael, Maria, and David, in Statesboro, Georgia, where James and Michael recently earned the rank of Eagle.

The Conners family stays busy in the outdoors by camping and day-hiking in the local state parks, backpacking on the Appalachian Trail, and kayaking on the region's lakes and rivers . . . when they aren't writing cookbooks!

Visit Tim and Christine at www.lipsmackincampin.com for recipes and tips and on YouTube at CampCookingTV for video instructionals.